# LANG

By

## Mildred A. Dawson
## Jonnie Mashburn Miller

Published by
### WORLD BOOK COMPANY
Yonkers-on-Hudson
New York

# U A G E

## FOR DAILY USE

### GRADE
5

Illustrated by

CARL H. BENDER          WALTER BEACH HUMPHREY

E. JOSEPH DREANY        HARRY LEES

THEODORE C. EWEN        REVERE F. WISTEHUFF

## ACKNOWLEDGMENTS

For permission to reprint copyrighted material, grateful acknowledgment is made to the following publishers and authors:

*Child Life:* "Moving" by Eunice Tietjens.

Doubleday & Co., Inc.: "Sun and Moon" from *Fairies and Friends* by Rose Fyleman. Copyright, 1926, by Doubleday & Co., Inc.

Henry Holt & Co., Inc.: "The Fog" from *Chicago Poems* by Carl Sandburg. Copyright, 1916, by Henry Holt & Co. Copyright, 1943, by Carl Sandburg.

Houghton Mifflin Company: Selection from "The First Snowfall" by James Russell Lowell.

*Junior Natural History Magazine:* A book review of *Come, Jack!* by Robert W. McCulloch.

J. B. Lippincott Company: "Dandelion," reprinted by permission of the publishers from *Poems by a Little Girl* by Hilda Conkling. Copyright, 1920, by J. B. Lippincott Company.

The Macmillan Company: "In Praise of Dust" from *The Pointed People* by Rachel Field.

Rinehart & Co., Inc.: Adaptations from *The Hurricane's Children, Tales from Your Neck o' the Woods.* Copyright, 1937, by Carl Carmer and reprinted by permission of Rinehart & Company, Inc.

*Story Parade:* "I Met a Giant" by Valine Hobbs.

DM:LDU:FIVE–2

# TABLE OF CONTENTS

UNIT                                                              PAGE

**I   Getting Started**                                    **1**

Why You Need Language,  1
Using This Book,  6
Using Your Voice Well,  7
Expressing Ideas in Sentences,  8
Telling a Complete Thought,  11
Your Classroom Library,  13
Holding Discussions,  15
Building Your Vocabulary,  16
A Language Notebook,  18
Correct Pronunciation,  19
Checking Language Habits,  20
Spelling Demons,  21
How Well Do You Read?  22
Using Your Dictionary,  34
Checking a Written Lesson,  36
Writing a Paragraph,  38
Checking Spelling,  39
Writing Proper Names,  40
Filling Blanks Correctly,  41
Writing Capital Letters,  42
Using Punctuation Marks,  43

**II   Reading and Telling Stories**                **45**

Reading a Folk Tale,  45
Discussing the Tale,  50
Planning a Story Hour,  53
Is Your Story Interesting?  54
Using *Said* Correctly,  56

[ v ]

Outlining Your Story,  57
*Began* and *Begun*,  58
Exploring Your Dictionary,  59
Speaking to an Audience,  60
A Radio Play,  61
A Radio Program,  69
Using Your Voice Well,  70
An Original Tall Tale,  72
A Book of Original Tales,  76
Understanding Sentences,  77
Combining Short Sentences,  82
Writing Complete Sentences,  84
Writing Conversation,  86
How Well Do You Remember?  88
If You Need Help,  90

III  Conversation                              93

Talking about Hobbies,  93
What to Talk About,  99
Courtesies in Conversation,  102
Using the Correct Verb,  104
Improving Your Conversation,  106
Overworked Words,  107
Table Conversation,  108
Answering a Question,  110
Greetings and Good-bys,  112
Carrying a Message,  114
Receiving a Caller,  116
Making Introductions,  118
Conversation by Telephone,  119
Speaking Clearly,  122
Taking a Telephone Message,  124
How Well Do You Remember?  125
If You Need Help,  126

IV  Enjoying Books                                      129

Books of Long Ago,  129
Pronouncing Vowels Correctly,  134
Reading to Find Out,  136
Using an Encyclopedia,  137
Learning to Skim,  140
How the Library Helps You,  142
Giving a Book Report,  144
Using *A* and *An*,  149
Building a Book List,  150
Writing a Book Review,  152
Singular and Plural Nouns,  155
Writing Singular Possessives,  157
Writing Plural Possessives,  158
Applying for a Library Card,  159
A Radio Game,  160
How Well Do You Remember?  163
If You Need Help,  165

V  Making Reports                                       169

Celebrating Holidays,  169
Taking Notes,  172
Making an Outline,  174
Adding to Your Vocabulary,  175
Giving a Report,  176
Special Festivals,  179
Giving an Explanation,  182
Planning a Festival Book,  184
Writing for Information,  186
More Verb Forms,  187
Making Your Booklet,  188
A Holiday Program,  189
How Well Do You Remember?  189
If You Need Help,  190

UNIT                                                       PAGE

**VI**   Organizing a Club                                    **193**

Talking It Over,   193

Electing Officers,   196

Holding a Club Meeting,   198

Writing the Minutes,   200

Planning Committee Work,   203

Presenting a Committee Report,   204

Speaking Correctly,   205

Courtesy to a Speaker,   206

Making a Motion,   208

Making a Community Folder,   210

Correct Verb Forms,   215

Giving a Club Skit,   216

How Well Do You Remember?   218

If You Need Help,   218

**VII**   Writing Letters                                          **221**

A Letter from China,   221

Paper for Letter Writing,   225

A Letter of Request,   226

Addressing an Envelope,   228

Checking Business Letters,   229

A Trip to the Post Office,   232

*Gave* and *Given*,   234

*Sit* and *Sat*,   235

Reading a Friendly Letter,   236

Checking Friendly Letters,   237

Improving Sentences,   238

Using the Verb *Set*,   239

Sending a Package,   240

A "Thank-You" Letter,   241

Placing an Order,   242

Writing a Postal Card,   244

Dividing Words,   245

[ viii ]

Learning New Words,  246
A Note of Invitation,  248
Answering Invitations,  249
How Well Do You Remember?  250
If You Need Help,  251

VIII   Writing for Fun                                                         253
Stories of Everyday Life,  253
A New Use for Commas,  258
Improving What You Write,  259
Other Kinds of Stories,  260
Writing a Description,  262
Sharing What You Write,  263
Rhythm in Poetry,  264
Painting Word Pictures,  267
Using Comparisons,  268
Poems for Fun,  269
A Poem of Your Own,  271

IX   A Review Unit                                                             273

Index                                                                         301

# Unit One

## GETTING STARTED

## WHY YOU NEED LANGUAGE

One morning the members of Miss Allison's class were startled almost out of their chairs. It was that Henry Bates again. Henry was always saying something that nobody else would ever dare to say.

"Miss Allison," began Henry, "I'm going to be a garage mechanic when I grow up. I know enough language already for that kind of work. I see why I need to study arithmetic, but it seems to me that studying language is a lot of foolishness."

No wonder the class were wide-eyed. Just imagine telling a teacher that studying language is a lot of foolishness!

"That's a fair statement," said Miss Allison. She knew that Henry was not trying to show off. He was merely repeating what he had heard others say, and he was perfectly sincere about it.

"I have an idea," Miss Allison went on. "Suppose all of you tell what you plan to do when you grow

[ 1 ]

up, and how language will help you do it. Would you like to begin, Bob?"

"I want to be an airplane pilot," announced Bob. "A pilot must plan each trip. In order to do that, he must be able to read all kinds of maps, charts, and directions. While in the air, he must talk with the radio operator and give and take important instructions. If his plane is forced down because of bad weather, he must get in touch with the flight engineer at his home field and get information about hotels and about train and bus schedules in the community where he lands. Just think! People's lives may depend upon how well I speak and understand the English language."

"A doctor should know how to speak well, too," said Jack. "If he doesn't, his directions to patients and nurses may not be clear."

"We should hear from one of the girls now," suggested Miss Allison. "How about you, Doris?"

"When I grow up, I want to get married and keep house," said Doris. The children all began to laugh, but Doris continued, "I don't see why being a housewife isn't just as important as being an airplane pilot or a doctor."

"Yes, but if you're going to wash dishes and sweep floors, you don't need to know anything about language," said Jerry.

"That's where you're wrong, Jerry," answered Doris. "I'll have to make out grocery lists and telephone orders to the stores. If I have somebody to

help me with the work, I'll have to explain just how she is to do the cooking or the cleaning."

"My mother says," remarked Nancy, "that there are so many improvements for making housework easy that women now have time for reading, writing letters, listening to the radio, and going to the theater. That means that they need to be able to understand the language of others if they wish to make the most of these things."

"Abraham Lincoln didn't have an education," Henry interrupted, "and look what he did. He didn't have to go to school and waste an hour every day studying language. Yet he was a fine President, and he made one of the greatest speeches of all time."

"Lincoln studied at night," said Doris quickly. "I remember a picture in a book that showed him lying before a log fire reading a book."

"Yes, but he studied because he liked to. He didn't have to do it," objected Henry.

"But, Henry, the point is that he *did* study and he *did* have an education, even if he got most of it from reading books all by himself," reminded Nancy.

"Nancy's right," said Miss Allison. "Lincoln studied at night when he must have been very tired after a long day of farm labor. How many of you would have the courage to do that? I know I wouldn't."

[ 4 ]

I. In the conversation you have just read, what kinds of work were mentioned? What different uses of language were suggested?

II. Which of the children thought of language as a help in expressing their own ideas? Who thought of language as a way of getting ideas from others, either by listening or by reading?

III. Discuss with your classmates what you expect to do when you grow up. Tell them how you will use language in following your chosen work. Think carefully before you speak, so that you will use words correctly and build them into good, clear sentences. Express your ideas as well as you can. Listen to others so that you may gather their ideas.

IV. After you have finished your conversation, answer these questions:

1. Did each speaker have interesting thoughts to express?
2. Did some find it hard to choose the right words and build good sentences?
3. Did anyone use incorrect words?
4. Did everyone speak clearly enough for all to hear?

Your conversation is a good test of your language ability. Does it show that you need to improve your power to choose the right words? build better sentences? speak more correctly?

[ 5 ]

## USING THIS BOOK

Did your class conversation show that you all need help in improving your language? See how this book can help you.

I. Turn to the *table of contents* of this book. On what pages is there a unit on *Conversation?* Read the lesson titles. Which lessons have help for you?

II. Is it hard for you to decide whether to use *wasn't* or *weren't? spoke* or *spoken? good* or *well?* Find these words in the *index* of this book. On what pages will you find help with each word?

In the index find the topic *Usage, correct.* Look through the long list of words under it. Someday you may need help with these words.

III. Find *Sentences* in the index. On what pages can you find help with writing complete sentences?

IV. Since this book is to be a good friend, use it carefully. Here are some things to remember.

---

### HOW TO HANDLE YOUR BOOK

1. Do not write in this book.
2. Turn a page by grasping the upper corner. Do not moisten your fingers.
3. Use a bookmark to keep a place.
4. Do not soil or tear this book.

---

# USING YOUR VOICE WELL

When you listen to your favorite radio programs, do you notice the voices of the announcers and of the actors or speakers? Voice training is important to a radio announcer. A radio voice must be pleasant to hear and it must carry well. It must put meaning and feeling into words and sentences; that is, it must be *expressive*.

I. Below is a list of words that might be used to describe the voices that you hear every day. Choose from the list those words that describe voices you like to hear. Use your dictionary to find the meaning of any word that is new to you. Use each word in a sentence of your own.

| | | |
|---|---|---|
| clear | nasal | lifeless |
| harsh | loud | strong |
| pleasing | strident | expressive |
| musical | lively | well-rounded |
| shrill | singsong | soft |

II. Make a class list of words that describe the kind of voice each of you should try to use when you speak to the class during the year. You may include some of the words listed above. Add other describing words of your own.

III. Choose a story from your reader. Let each pupil read aloud several sentences from the story. The class will judge whether each reader's voice can be described by the words you listed. If it cannot, tell him in what ways he needs to improve his voice.

# EXPRESSING IDEAS IN SENTENCES

During a school day, you ask and answer many questions. You hold conversations, have discussions, and make explanations. You read from books and you report what you read. You write lessons.

That is, all day you are either forming sentences to express what you have to say, or you are trying to understand the sentences of others. For this reason, the sentence is an important language tool.

In this lesson you will review what you have learned about the sentence.

## Kinds of sentences

You express your ideas in different kinds of sentences, such as these:

*Statement:* The *Essex* is an airplane carrier.
*Question:* How many planes does it carry?
*Command or request:* Tell how carrier planes land.

Sometimes you make your voice show strong feeling when you express a thought. You may say:

What a great ship that is!

You try to express the wonder you feel. Such a sentence is an *exclamatory* (ex·clam'a·to·ry) sentence. Here are some other exclamatory sentences:

It carries over eighty planes! (expresses surprise)
See that plane land! (expresses excitement)

Read each of these sentences aloud and make your voice show the feeling you want it to express.

[ 8 ]

## Writing sentences

When you speak, your voice and manner of speaking help to make your sentences clear. But when you write, you must follow rules for capitalization and punctuation, or you will have a jumble of words that no one can understand. Review these rules for writing sentences.

---

### HOW TO WRITE A SENTENCE

1. Begin the first word with a capital letter.
2. Put a period after a statement or a command.
3. Put a question mark after a question.
4. Put an exclamation point after a sentence that expresses strong feeling.

---

If you make a habit of checking every sentence you write against these rules, your written lessons will be easy for others to read.

## Practice with Sentences

1. To prove to yourself that you can follow the rules on page 9, write these sentences correctly:

1. who were the first passengers to ride in a balloon
2. believe it or not, they were a lamb, a duck, and a rooster
3. two Frenchmen, the Montgolfier brothers, made a balloon that went up 6000 feet
4. it was a cloth bag lined with paper
5. what kept it afloat
6. it was filled with smoke
7. how the people laughed when they first saw it
8. the passengers rode in a basket that hung below the bag
9. why were there no human passengers
10. no one wanted to risk his life
11. the balloon remained in the air for eight minutes
12. what a surprise that was to the people who had laughed

2. What have you read about the first successful airplane flight of the Wright brothers? Write four good sentences about this flight — a statement, a question, a command, and an exclamatory sentence,

# TELLING A COMPLETE THOUGHT

Do you know the difference between a sentence and a group of words that does not form a sentence? Take these exercises to find out. Remember:

A sentence expresses a complete thought.

1. Here are ten groups of words, placed in pairs. In each pair one group is a sentence and one group is not a sentence. Write each complete sentence.

1. When the weather is foggy, or when it is raining heavily.
   In bad weather an airplane pilot can land by "riding the beam."
2. "Riding the beam" means following a radio signal.
   Until the plane is safe on the ground.
3. If he is "on the beam," there is a constant buzzing in his ears.
   Also repeating the name of the station once each minute.
4. The letter *A* if he is to the right of his course.
   If he is to the left of his course, he hears the letter *N*.
5. In order to land safely, a pilot must watch the wind.
   Watching the wind.

2. Make a sentence of each group of words above that is not a sentence. You may need to add words or to change words around.

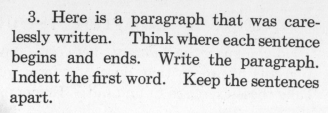

3. Here is a paragraph that was carelessly written. Think where each sentence begins and ends. Write the paragraph. Indent the first word. Keep the sentences apart.

Have you ever seen a helicopter it is a queer-looking aircraft it has whirling wings over its body the helicopter does not require a runway it can rise straight up from the ground another queer thing is that it can stand still while in the air

4. Write a short paragraph about something interesting that you heard or read this week. Be sure to keep your sentences apart with capital letters and periods.

## SENTENCE SUMMARY

Here is a summary of what you need to remember about the sentence.

1. *A sentence expresses a complete thought.* In other words, *a sentence makes sense.* A group of words that does not make sense is not a sentence.

2. A written sentence must begin with a capital letter and end with some mark of punctuation. When a number of sentences are written in a paragraph, the beginning and ending of each sentence must be clearly marked.

[ 12 ]

You already know that reading books is an important part of language work.

Are there shelves of books in your room? Is there an encyclopedia? Is there a large dictionary? Take a short period of time to get acquainted with your class library. Learn what books there are and where they are.

I. Hold a discussion about your class library. Discuss these questions:

1. Are the books so arranged that you can find any one that you need?
2. Are the encyclopedia and dictionary where you can use them with ease?
3. Do any books need mending?
4. Would you like more books or more kinds of books?

As you discuss, make a list of the ways in which you can improve your class library. The picture on page 17 may suggest ideas to you.

II. Choose committees to carry out your plans. You may need them for the following purposes:

> For getting extra shelves
> For arranging books
> For mending books
> For finding where to get more books

List the members of the different committees and put the lists on your bulletin board.

# ARRANGING LIBRARY SHELVES

The following exercises will help a committee arrange the books on your library shelves:

I. While visiting the Children's Room in a public library, you may have learned that books of one kind are grouped on shelves or sets of shelves. The shelves are labeled to show the kinds of books on them. Here are some of the labels that you may have read:

| | | |
|---|---|---|
| History | Poetry | Geography |
| Science | Fiction | Biography |
| Travel | Health | Reference Books |

If you do not know what some of these names mean, discuss them. What kinds of books would be grouped under *Science? Fiction? Biography? Reference Books?*

II. The books of one kind are placed on the shelf or shelves in alphabetical order by the authors' last names. Because of this arrangement, it is important for you to know the name of the author of the book for which you are looking.

On a history shelf you may find books by the following authors:

Kelty   Beeby   Chapman   Tryon   Guerber

Tell the order in which you would find books by these authors if you began at the left of the shelf.

III. If you are not sure of the order of letters in the alphabet, review them now.

# HOLDING DISCUSSIONS

You hold a class discussion in order to talk over class problems and to decide how to solve them. Unless each person does his share and does it well, a discussion is a waste of time. Judge your library discussion by these standards.

---

## STANDARDS FOR DISCUSSIONS

1. Discuss points of importance to the group.
2. Keep to the subject as each point is discussed.
3. Allow everyone to express his opinion.
4. Decide what opinions the largest number of the group hold.
5. Make plans to solve the problems raised.

---

Each girl and boy can check his part in the discussion by asking himself these questions:

1. Did I think before I spoke?
2. Did I take only my fair share of the time, or did I talk too much?
3. Did I express my thoughts as well as I could?
4. Did I speak clearly and loudly enough so that all could hear?
5. Did I use words correctly?

You are likely to have many class discussions during the year. Come back to this page often and use these standards and checks. Try to improve your discussion.

# BUILDING YOUR VOCABULARY

When you were six years old, you could probably use about four or five thousand words. How did you get this stock of words, or *vocabulary*? You heard other people use words, and you imitated what they said.

How do you add to your vocabulary now? You still learn many words by ear. That is, you hear people speak, and you listen to the radio. But you also learn many new words by reading good books.

Like the sentence, the *word* is an important tool of language. You need words to build sentences. Be a "word scout." Keep your ears and eyes open for new words to add to your vocabulary.

I. When you read the conversation on pages 1–4, did you find any new words? Turn to those pages. Read them again. List the new words you would like to learn. Use each in a sentence of your own.

II. If you read carefully, you found ten words you might use in place of the overworked word *said:* page 1, *began, went on;* page 2, *announced, suggested, continued, answered;* page 3, *remarked, interrupted;* page 4, *objected, reminded.*

Make your language more interesting by using some of these words in place of *said.* Use each one of them now in a sentence.

III. Be on the lookout for more interesting words to use in place of some overworked words you now use. On the blackboard make a list of words to use in place of *came;* of *saw;* of *got;* of *went.*

[ 16 ]

# A LANGUAGE NOTEBOOK

Start a Language Notebook. Your teacher will help you to plan the right kind.

Divide your notebook into sections. From time to time this book will give you suggestions about what to put in your notebook.

Head the first page of section one Vocabulary. Every time you read or hear a new word that you like, write it in your notebook. Be sure to master the word by learning how to pronounce it, what it means, and how to spell it. Then write it in your notebook in this way:

WORD        MEANING        SENTENCE
*startled*    *surprised*    *Henry's speech startled*
                             *the children.*

If you have made up your mind to be a word scout, leave enough pages in your Language Notebook for all the new words you wish to use.

# CORRECT PRONUNCIATION

Do you mispronounce some common words that you use often? You may not need the dictionary to set you straight on such words. What you need to do is to break careless habits of speech. These exercises will help you break some of these bad habits:

1. Pronounce each syllable of these words:

ge·og′ra·phy (*not* "jog er phy")
a·rith′me·tic (*not* "rith me tic")
his′to·ry     (*not* "his try")
fi′nal·ly     (*not* "fine ly")
prob′a·bly    (*not* "prob ly")
re′al·ly      (*not* "ree ly")

2. Do you carelessly add a syllable in any of the following words? Pronounce each word:

drowned        (*not* "drown ded")
at·tacked′     (*not* "at tack ted")
ath′lete       (*not* "ath a lete")
film           (*not* "fil um")
um·brel′la     (*not* "um ber el la")
mis′chie·vous (*not* "mis chie vi ous")

3. Say each word, watching the underlined part:

o′ver·alls (*not* "o ver halls")
chil′dren  (*not* "chil dern")
hun′dred   (*not* "hun derd")
ga·losh′es (*not* "goo losh es")
ex′tra     (*not* "ex try")
col′umn    (*not* "col yum")

[ 19 ]

## CHECKING LANGUAGE HABITS

On this page and on later pages, you will find check tests. They will help you find out how well you remember what you have learned about correct speech and writing in earlier grades.

### Check Test 1: Correct Words

Copy the following story. Be sure to choose the correct word from those in parentheses.

#### MY GHOST STORY

One night Catherine and I (went, gone) past the old graveyard on our way to church. Old Ben had just told us a story about a ghost that (run, ran) after children. Of course, we have never (saw, seen) a ghost. But we had never (went, gone) past the graveyard at night before.

Just as we reached the graveyard, we (saw, seen) a tall figure in white. As we watched, it (come, came) toward us. We (did, done) just what you would have (did, done). Never had we (run, ran) so fast before!

After we got to church, Aunt Alice (come, came) in, dressed all in white. She told us she had (come, came) through the graveyard. We have never (saw, seen) a ghost since.

Remember to edit your paper before you hand it in. If you miss any words in this test, study page 280.

# SPELLING DEMONS

You probably have a short period each day in which you study spelling or write a spelling lesson. Perhaps you have a perfect score in your regular spelling lessons.

But you are not perfect in spelling unless you spell correctly all words in every written lesson. Do you check the spelling of every word you write?

Most boys and girls are bothered by certain words every time they write them. Do words such as *to*, *two*, and *too*, *by* and *buy*, *read* and *reed*, or *believe* and *receive* trouble you?

Do you do such silly things as to write "gril" for *girl*, or "Jhon" for *John*, or "whent" for *went?*

Decide what your spelling demons are. In your Language Notebook head section two Spelling Demons. List there the words that are hard for you and the words in which you make mistakes. Study these words daily and practice writing them in sentences. Have someone check your practice.

Spell correctly every word you write in your daily lessons.

Make a habit of turning to your dictionary and checking the spelling of any word of which you are not sure.

In this way you will soon master the words that cause you trouble in your written lessons.

[ 21 ]

# HOW WELL DO YOU READ?

Here is the story of a boy who was determined to be a good pilot.   As you read it, try to get the meaning of each new word.   Fit the meaning into the sentence. Keep your eyes open for interesting details.   See what happens in the story and why.

## READY TO SOLO

As Ken Williams finished his lunch at the Winston airport, he could see his training plane being refueled. Beside him sat Mr. Gray, his flying instructor at the Gateway Flying School.   With Ken at the stick, they had flown the sixty miles between Winston and Gateway and were resting before flying back.

Ken eyed the sturdy little monoplane fondly.   If he made a perfect take-off, he felt sure Mr. Gray would recommend him for his solo flight tomorrow. Ken had always dreamed of being a pilot.   Would his dream come true tomorrow?

"Let's look at the flight map between Winston and Gateway," said Mr. Gray.

In the map room Ken studied the aerial wall map carefully.   "If I follow that stretch of railroad track

to the right of Mount Baldy," he said, "it will take me straight to Gateway."

"You're a good navigator, Ken," said Mr. Gray. "You won't need me much longer."

Then Ken and Mr. Gray picked up their parachutes in the office and went out to the waiting plane.

Slipping into the pilot's seat, Ken fastened his safety belt and studied the instrument panel.

"Gas on, switch off, throttle closed!" he called.

A mechanic spun the propeller. "Contact!"

"Contact!" repeated Ken, snapping on the switch.

Then he opened the throttle, and the motor roared. As he gave the signal, a man pulled the chocks from under the landing wheels, and Ken taxied to the line.

Heading the ship into the wind, Ken waited his turn to take off. Sometimes he had trouble with the take-off. But this one had to be perfect.

As Ken widened the throttle, the plane rolled down the runway, gathering speed. The wind lifted the plane from the ground, and Ken eased back on the stick, smiling to himself.

But, as the plane began to climb, a sudden cross wind caught at the left wing. By using the rudder pedals and the stick, Ken quickly righted the ship. It climbed steadily upward, but Ken's heart did not rise with it. It wasn't his fault that the take-off had been sloppy. But would Mr. Gray know that?

Ken was too busy flying the ship to worry for long. When his altimeter read 2000 feet, he leveled off. A cross wind was forcing him off his course.

[ 23 ]

"Like swimming across a river current," Ken said to Mr. Gray as he checked the compass for direction. He was glad Mr. Gray had reminded him to take on extra gas at Winston. He would need it if he had to fight a cross wind all the way to Gateway.

Ken didn't settle back in his seat until Mount Baldy loomed up on his right. The mountain was an important check point. After that, it was easy to pick out the twin strips of railroad track that cut through the checkerboard of green and golden fields. By following them, he flew straight to Gateway.

At Gateway, Ken circled the school's flying field for a look at the wind sock. It showed that there was a strong south wind. So Ken circled the field again before he fell in behind another training plane and set his ship down in a perfect three-point landing.

After taxiing the ship to the hangar for the ground crew to check, Ken went to the office to fill out his logbook. Mr. Gray and the Chief Instructor met him at the door.

"From the way you set that ship down, it looks as though you're about ready to solo, Ken," said the Chief Instructor. "Mr. Gray, is Ken ready to fly without you?"

Ken held his breath as Mr. Gray answered. "I'll leave that up to Ken, Chief. If he thinks he's ready, let him solo."

Ken met Mr. Gray's piercing blue eyes. "I think I'm ready, Mr. Gray," he said.

"We'll see you tomorrow then," smiled the Chief.

"I couldn't have ordered a better day," grinned Ken as he climbed into the cockpit of his plane the next day. "The weatherman says ceiling and visibility unlimited," he added, fastening the straps of his parachute, "and that wind sock out there is as limp as a dishrag."

"No, you won't have to fight wind today," said Mr. Gray. He had stepped up on the wing as Ken checked the instruments. "Maybe you'll set some kind of record, Ken. I'm going to time you. And now how about a nice, clean take-off for me?"

He stepped back with a friendly wave of his hand as the mechanic spun the propeller.

Ken watched for other planes as he rolled down the level runway.

"I'll make Mr. Gray proud of my take-off yet," he promised himself.

With Mr. Gray watching him, Ken was glad that his take-off was smooth and even. But he knew it was too early to relax. He had a lot of miles to fly before he would prove to Mr. Gray that he could handle a plane alone.

Cruising over the beautiful summer countryside, with the plane in perfect control, Ken felt as happy as a king.

"Maybe I will set a record," he thought as he noticed that he was hitting most of the check points ahead of the schedule he had worked out yesterday.

Almost before he knew it, he was approaching the Winston airport. He checked his gas gauge. There was more than enough gas for a return flight. He would save time if he didn't bother to refuel his plane.

But he seemed to hear Mr. Gray's warning, "You won't find a filling station upstairs."

"Maybe I won't set any records," Ken told himself, "but if I have enough gas I won't have to set the plane down in a hayfield."

When he glided down out of the cool sky onto the hot runway, he turned his plane over to the ground crew for refueling.

"You won't be sorry," the mechanic told him. "It's only beginners who try to skimp on gas."

After his logbook was signed at the Winston office, Ken hurried back to the line. When his plane was refueled and ready, he took off like a homing pigeon.

"I wish Mr. Gray could have seen *that* take-off," he smiled as he leveled off at 2000 feet.

When Mount Baldy rose on his right, Ken thought the rugged mountain looked like an old friend.

As the mountain fell behind him, Ken spotted a train puffing along the railroad tracks below him.

"I have plenty of gas," Ken thought for a moment. "I guess I'll go down and buzz that train."

"A good pilot is never a show-off, Ken," Mr. Gray's words seemed to ring in his ear. It was almost as if his instructor were in the cockpit with him.

"You're right, Mr. Gray," said Ken aloud. "I can't afford to make any foolish mistakes today."

The train had disappeared around the bend at the foot of Old Baldy before Ken checked the railroad tracks again. For a moment he thought he was seeing double. A curl of smoke was rising along the track.

"That doesn't look like train smoke," Ken thought.

Putting the ship into a steep bank, he circled the smoking spot. He could see that the smoke was coming from a fire in the thick, dry grass along the track. It had started, no doubt, from a live spark from the passing train.

Ken cut his engine and came in closer. The fire was spreading slowly to the stubble of a near-by wheat field. Ken knew that the first breath of a breeze would carry it to the shocks of ripened wheat.

Ramming the throttle all the way forward, Ken nosed the plane upward. A half mile to the north he could see a big, comfortable farmhouse. In a near-by hayfield a baling machine was busily at work.

"I've got to get word to those men at once," Ken thought desperately   "But how?"

As though in answer to his own question, Ken started the plane on a long, slow glide toward the noisy baler.

When his altimeter read 500 feet, he leaned out of the cockpit. "Fire!" he screamed, pointing to the end of the wheat field.

A few men stopped their work to wave, but most of them did not even look up. They were used to seeing student pilots from the Gateway Flying School.

"They think I'm just a show-off," thought Ken as he pulled the ship up into a steep climb and circled high over the field for another dive.

But, as he leveled off, he knew that there wasn't time for another dive. Hovering high over the far end of the field, Ken made up his mind swiftly. He would land his plane on the hayfield. He could see that it was level, and he knew that the net of underground roots would make it solid.

Ken kept his eye on all his instruments as he glided in over the long stretch of field. When he felt all three wheels touch and hold the ground, he smiled. Then he bumped along to a stop within one hundred feet of the dusty baler.

"What are you trying to do?" called an old man, as he ran, his straw hat in his hand, toward Ken in the quivering plane.

Ken leaned out of the cockpit. "I've been trying to tell you your wheat field is on fire. . . ."

In a few minutes the farm jeep, loaded with men, shovels, and wet sacks, was headed for the fire. Watching them go, Ken sank back in his seat and wiped his brow.

"Whew! I made a forced landing. If I'd thought about it, I might have been scared," he told himself with a relieved grin.

Throttling down his engine, he checked his plane over carefully. He hadn't damaged his wheels in landing on the rough field, and he still had plenty of gas. There wasn't any good reason why he shouldn't take off. On the other hand, he sometimes had trouble taking off. . . .

Maybe he had better call the school and tell Mr. Gray what had happened. Mr. Gray was used to driving out and picking up students who had been forced down.

"That was mighty neighborly of you to set down in our hayfield and tell us about the fire," said the old man as the jeep disappeared across the field. "You know, my boy has been wanting to take flying lessons, but I've been against it until now. If you take off from this field, I may have to change my mind."

Once more Ken made a quick decision. "If you'll check the ground ahead of me for rocks and holes, I'll show you how simple it is," he said.

When the old man gave the signal and stepped aside, Ken opened the throttle and rolled over the bumpy ground. Faster. Faster! Then the air slid in under the wings and lifted the plane aloft.

Easing back on the stick, Ken climbed into the wide, blue sky. Dipping once over the railroad track, he saw that the farmers had the fire under control.

Then, with a heart as free as a bird's, Ken followed the tracks to Gateway. He had not only made his own dream come true. He had helped the dream of another boy come true, too.

When he set the ship down on the flying-school field, Mr. Gray was waiting for him, watch in hand.

"You didn't break any records, Ken," he smiled. "But at least I didn't have to come after you."

Ken laughed out loud. "How much time am I allowed for making a forced landing in a hayfield?"

When Mr. Gray heard the whole story, he nodded. "You were right about being ready to solo, Ken."

"I'm glad you think so, sir," grinned Ken.

[ 32 ]

I. Did you enjoy the story? Can you tell what happened from the time Ken left the Winston airport on his solo flight until he returned to Gateway?

If you are not sure, perhaps it is because you did not understand some of the words or sentences. Pilots often use strange words and expressions. If you do not know what they mean, you may not enjoy stories about flying.

See whether some of the boys and girls in the class can explain these expressions:

a perfect take-off
a solo flight
a flight map
gas on, switch off, throttle closed
leveled off
a perfect three-point landing
ceiling and visibility unlimited
a filling station upstairs
buzz the train
putting the ship into a steep bank

II. Here are other terms you need to know if you wish to read aviation stories. Do you know what these terms mean?

| | | |
|---|---|---|
| monoplane | ground crew | wind sock |
| cockpit | forced landing | chocks |
| parachute | stick | rudder pedals |
| instrument panel | mechanic | altimeter |
| navigator | logbook | gas gauge |

# USING YOUR DICTIONARY

If you do not know the meaning of a word listed on page 33, your dictionary can help you. Suppose that you need help with the word *altimeter*. Find it in your own dictionary. You will see something like this:

al·tim′e·ter (ăl·tĭm′ĕ·tẽr). An instrument for measuring the height at which an aircraft is flying

I. How many syllables has this word? Say each syllable aloud. Knowing the syllables will help you to pronounce and to spell the word correctly.

II. What helps in pronunciation do you find? First, there is the *accent mark*. What does it tell you?

In parentheses ( ), you see the word again, this time with marks over the letters *a*, *i*, and *e*. The marks tell you how to sound these letters. This year you will learn what some of these marks mean.

Say *altimeter* after your teacher says it.

III. Read the meaning of the word.

IV. Learn the spelling of the word. It is easy if you learn to spell each syllable.

Let your dictionary help you to increase the number of new words in your vocabulary. You can learn from the dictionary how to divide a word into syllables, how to pronounce it, what it means, and how to spell it.

Do not write a word in your Language Notebook until you know these four things about it.

## Dictionary Practice

1. With your thumbs, divide your dictionary into three equal parts. What letters of the alphabet are in the first part? the middle part? the last part? See how quickly you can tell in which part you will find each of these words:

compass       safety belt    propeller
throttle      gauge          airport
taxi          logbook        baler
hangar        altitude       instructor

2. Name the words above in alphabetical order.

3. The guide words on one dictionary page are *doily* and *donation*. Which of the following words will you find on that page?

dollar      donkey      dock      domino

4. Find each word in exercise 1 in your dictionary. Read its meaning.

5. Write these words in alphabetical order. You will need to look beyond the fourth letter to do it.

aviator       altitude       airport       altimeter

6. Here are more words from the story "Ready to Solo" on pages 22–32. See how quickly you can find each one in your dictionary and read its meaning.

schedule      current       glided       recommend
decision      loomed        skimp        aerial
cruising      relax         chocks       course

# CHECKING A WRITTEN LESSON

In which subjects do you write papers to hand in? How do you usually head these papers?

I. Look at the written lesson on the next page. What facts are given in the heading? Give a rule for each capital letter and punctuation mark used. Is the abbreviation for September correct? Check by your dictionary.

Ask your teacher to plan with you the right heading for your papers.

II. Are there good margins on all four sides of Jerry's paper? Is the title of the report written correctly? Is each paragraph indented? Does each sentence begin and end correctly?

Check your written lessons by asking these questions.

---

### CHECKS FOR A WRITTEN LESSON

1. Is the heading correct? Have I used capital letters correctly? Did I place a comma between the day and the year?
2. Have I kept good margins on all sides?
3. Is my handwriting neat and readable?
4. Is each sentence a complete thought?
5. Did I begin and end each sentence correctly?
6. Have I spelled all words correctly?

---

## How a Plane Flies

An airplane can fly because it has a propeller and wings. The propeller pulls the plane forward. The wings help it to rise and stay aloft.

The motor turns the propeller blades. These blades cut into the air and pull the plane forward.

The front edges of the wings are tilted upward. When air hits these edges very fast, it is sucked under the wings and pushes the plane up.

When the air rushes over the curved surface of the wings, it pulls strongly on the wing tops. This pull of air at the top of the plane helps to keep the plane in the air.

# WRITING A PARAGRAPH

Betty wrote this paragraph about her favorite doll:

## My Favorite Doll

My favorite doll is called Priscilla-Pocahontas. She is a rag doll with two heads. One head is made of white material. The other is made of brown material. When I hold up the white head, I have Priscilla in her colonial costume. When I hold up the brown head, I have Pocahontas, the beautiful Indian princess, in a beaded dress.

Did Betty indent the first line? Did she use capital letters and punctuation marks to keep her sentences apart?

Read a sentence from Betty's paragraph that tells the topic. Did Betty stick to that topic?

1. Write this paragraph and correct the errors: children of every land make dolls. Children who live near the sea sometimes make dolls of crab claws or shells and other children make dolls of spools or corncobs. in some countries girls make dolls from dough and bake them in the oven.

2. Write a paragraph of your own about any one of these topics:

My Favorite Toy     My Favorite Game
My Favorite Pet     My Favorite Holiday

# CHECKING SPELLING

When you read each paper before you hand it in, look closely for careless mistakes in spelling.

Find the misspelled word or words in each sentence below. Then write the sentence, spelling that word correctly. Use your dictionary if necessary.

1. I am shure Jack is coming.
2. We had a verry quite day.
3. The story tells about fourty theives.
4. We were haveing fun with are kitten.
5. The strom passed over quickly.
6. Bob made a find speach.
7. The poor gril was reddy to give up.

Exchange papers with a classmate. Check his paper while he checks yours.


## SOME TROUBLESOME WORDS

These pairs of words sound alike but are spelled differently:

| threw | their | so | led | red | right |
|-------|-------|-----|------|-----|-------|
| through | there | sew | lead | read | write |

Decide which groups of words give you trouble. Find each word in your dictionary and see how the meaning helps you to choose the right spelling. Then write sentences using the words.

Ask someone to check your paper. If you still miss words, list them among your Spelling Demons.

# WRITING PROPER NAMES

You have learned to begin some names with capital letters because they are special names. Such special names are called *proper* names. Look at these common and proper names:

| Common | Proper | Common | Proper |
|---|---|---|---|
| boy | Joseph | day | Friday |
| city | Cleveland | month | February |
| county | Dark County | holiday | Christmas |
| state | Idaho | street | Bond Street |
| country | China | school | Taft School |
| people | Chinese | library | Arden Library |

Learn this rule for writing proper names:

**Begin all proper names with capital letters.**

In each sentence below are one or more proper names. They should begin with capital letters. Write each sentence correctly on the blackboard.

1. Cowboys and indians live in the western part of the united states.
2. There are many cowboys and indians in idaho, nevada, and montana.
3. Each summer during july and august the cowboys put on shows called rodeos.
4. A big rodeo is held every year at cheyenne, wyoming.

[ 40 ]

# FILLING BLANKS CORRECTLY

On your first day at school this year, did your teacher ask you to fill out a card with your name and age? Perhaps you also gave your parents' names and address and your father's occupation.

At different times during the year, you will need to fill out special blanks and forms which ask for information. When you do, be sure to give all the information asked for. Print or write each part in the space provided for it.

Here is a heading from a reading test. Think what information you would write on each blank line.

NAME \_\_\_\_?\_\_\_\_ BOY OR GIRL \_\_\_?\_\_\_

DATE OF BIRTH \_\_\_?\_\_\_ GRADE \_\_\_?\_\_\_

TEACHER \_\_\_\_\_?\_\_\_\_\_

SCHOOL \_\_\_\_\_?\_\_\_\_\_

CITY \_\_\_?\_\_\_ DATE \_\_\_?\_\_\_

1. Make an exact copy of the blank above. Draw it twice the size it is shown in your book. Then fill out your copy of the blank correctly.

2. Bring to class a blank or form you find at home in a magazine or newspaper. Trim it neatly and fill it in carefully. A committee may select the best-filled forms and blanks and display them on the class bulletin board.

# WRITING CAPITAL LETTERS

Take the check test on this page. It will prove to you whether you are able to use capital letters correctly in your written work.

## Check Test 2: Capital Letters

If you do not have a perfect score on this test, find the help you need on pages 274–275.

1. Write correctly the name and address of your father and mother.

2. Write each sentence correctly, supplying capital letters where they are needed.

1. my birthday will be on the first tuesday in october.

2. my cousin tom has moved to albany, new york.

3. our dogs are named jock and sandy.

3. Where are capital letters needed in this book report? Write the paragraph correctly.

one of the best books i have ever read is *gigi: the story of a merry-go-round horse.* the book was written by elizabeth foster. although gigi loved all the children, he loved lili, his first rider, best of all. gigi traveled all over europe. finally he was sent to america.

# USING PUNCTUATION MARKS

Take the following check test to see how well you remember correct punctuation.

## Check Test 3: Punctuation

If you make errors in this test, turn to pages 276–277, where you will find a review of all the punctuation rules you have learned.

1. Write the following sentences correctly:
   1. Where shall we meet after school
   2. You may come to my house
   3. Bring Jerry with you
   4. What a fine camera you have

2. Each of these sentences contains a quotation. Write the sentence and put in the correct marks.
   1. Where do you live  asked Sue.
   2. Jane replied  I live on Bond Street.

3. Write these names correctly:

   Mr A E Collins       Mrs Thomas Parr

4. Write each sentence and put apostrophes where they are needed:
   1. Isnt that Dans mitt.
   2. I cant find my brothers book

5. Place periods after the abbreviations of:

   Friday    Tuesday    December    August

*Unit Two*

# READING AND TELLING STORIES

## READING A FOLK TALE

You will enjoy reading this folk tale from *The Hurricane's Children* by Carl Carmer:

### TONY BEAVER AND THE BUCKWHEAT CAKES

In the high West Virginia mountains, where the Eel River dashes down toward what mountain folk call "The Levels," lies the lumber camp of Tony Beaver. It's pretty hard to find. In the first place, not even the best map of West Virginia shows the course of Eel River; and, in the second place, the camp is deep in the woods. But if you want to find it very much, and if you set out into the mountains and use your imagination hard enough, you will get there.

There are folk in West Virginia who can tell a good many Tony Beaver stories without repeating themselves. In towns like Black Betsey, Jumping Branch,

[ 45 ]

and Sleepy Creek, the tale of Tony and the buckwheat pancakes holds the interest of everyone.

.    .    .    .    .    .    .    .    .

One time when Tony went to visit his grandma, she baked him some mighty fine buckwheat cakes. Granny's griddle was as big as a whole township; and when she got it good and hot, she bound big sides of bacon on Tony's feet and let him go skating on the griddle to grease it.

Tony ate a hundred cakes that day before he started in using syrup; and after that he ate a couple hundred more *with* syrup.

Granny was worried about him.  "You're getting

downright puny, Tony," she scolded. "What's wrong with you today?"

"I reckon I'm just not very hungry, Granny," Tony replied. "Would you mind it if I wrapped up the rest of the cakes and took them along home with me? I'll probably be terrible hungry by the time I walk home."

"Land sakes, Tony, of course I wouldn't mind," answered his grandma. "Do you think I want it worded about that I don't give my grandson enough to eat when he comes to visit me?"

Tony wrapped up the cakes and started out. He was just passing through a stretch of woods when he ran slap into that smart Brer Rabbit.

Brer Rabbit said, "I see you're totin' some of your grandma's buckwheat cakes. I got quite a few persimmons in this big package, and I've got a good idea. We'll just lay your pancakes and my persimmons out on a log — first a pancake and then a persimmon — and then I'll say a few spell words over them. That will make them turn into just twice as many, and we can have a feast."

Tony's walk had already made him hungry; so he agreed to follow out Brer Rabbit's idea. He began laying cakes on a fallen log, and Brer Rabbit began laying persimmons beside them. While they were at it, Brer Rabbit recited this rhyme:

> First a persimmon — then a cake;
> Don't let me get a tummy-ache!

When all the cakes and persimmons were laid out on the log, Brer Rabbit all of a sudden hollered out,

"Bingo!" He grabbed up all the cakes and persimmons and started to run off with them!

But Tony Beaver was too quick for him. Brer Rabbit was in the air on his first hop when Tony fetched him a lick that knocked him higher than a kite. The wind caught his big ears as if they were sails; and away Brer Rabbit went, sailing around all over West Virginia for seven days, dropping persimmons and pancakes all the while he was up there. All the boys and girls in the state got out baskets and barrels to catch them; and to this day, folks talk about the week it rained pancakes and persimmons on West Virginia.

[ 49 ]

# DISCUSSING THE TALE

I. Did you like this folk tale as well as fairy tales you have read? If you did, tell why. If you did not, name some fairy tales that you like better, and tell why you like them.

II. Many people like the Tony Beaver stories because they *exaggerate*, or tell about impossible people and the impossible things they do. In fairy tales, such things happen by magic. In folk tales like the one about Tony Beaver, the characters can do impossible things because they are bigger and stronger than other people.

Girls and boys usually like tales of exaggeration because they are funny, or ridiculous. Name other tales of exaggeration that you have read.

III. In each section of our country, some people have peculiar ways of saying things. Such words or expressions are called *dialect*. You may have been puzzled by some of the words and expressions you read in the Tony Beaver story. See whether you can explain what each of the following means. Tell how you would express the same meaning in correct language.

| | |
|---|---|
| mighty fine | downright puny |
| reckon | ran slap into |
| worded about | a few spell words |
| totin' | fetched him a lick |
| hollered out | terrible hungry |

# READING MORE FOLK TALES

Every country in the world has its folk tales. You have read folk tales of the European countries. The stories of Ali Baba, Aladdin, and Sindbad the Sailor are folk tales told by the people of Asia.

American folk tales are different from all others. They were probably first told around campfires after the lumberjacks, cotton pickers, or oil drillers had finished a hard day's work. Because these men were doing hard, rough work, they wove tales about powerful men who were able to perform great feats of strength and daring. So their heroes were not kings or golden-haired princesses or fairy godmothers who waved magic wands. The magic is there, however, in the impossible doings of the imaginary heroes.

There is also to be found in the American folk tale a great deal of humor — something that is not often found in a fairy tale. Boys and girls read them for no other reason than to laugh at them and to enjoy their ridiculous exaggerations.

I. If you live in a state or region where there are other imaginary heroes about whom tales have been woven, tell who they are and something about them.

II. You will enjoy reading other tall tales about imaginary American heroes. If you cannot find more Tony Beaver stories, perhaps you can find books of tales about Paul Bunyan, the famous lumberman of the North; Kemp Morgan, the Oklahoma oil driller; Pecos Bill, the cowboy of the Southwest;

Mike Fink, of the Mississippi and Ohio Valleys; John Henry, the giant railroad worker; and Uncle Remus of the South, who told the Brer Rabbit tales.

See whether your class, school, or public library has any of these books:

*Cape Cod Pilot*, by Josef Berger
*Tall Tale America*, by Walter Blair
*Nights with Uncle Remus*, by Joel Chandler Harris
*John Henry*, by Guy Johnson
*Yankee Doodle's Cousins*, by Anne Malcolmson
*Tall Timber Tales*, by Dell J. McCormick
*Pecos Bill and Lightning*, by Leigh Peck
*How Old Stormalong Captured Mocha Dick*, by Irwin Shapiro
*Yankee Thunder; The Legendary Life of Davy Crockett*, by Irwin Shapiro
*Paul Bunyan*, by Esther Shephard
*Paul Bunyan, the Work Giant*, by Ida V. Turney
*Paul Bunyan and His Great Blue Ox*, by Wallace Wadsworth

Most of the stories in these books you can easily read yourself. If you find some of them difficult because of hard words or strange dialect, perhaps your teacher or an older friend will read them to you.

As you learn about the many different imaginary heroes of America, choose the one you like best. Try to find as many tales about him as you can. In your Language Notebook list the titles of the tales and the books from which they came.

# PLANNING A STORY HOUR

When you have all had time to read some good American folk tales, plan a weekly Story Hour when you may tell some of the best tall tales you have read. Would you like to have a separate hour for the stories of each section of our country? If you would, the suggestions that follow will help you to prepare for your story hours:

I. Discuss plans for your Story Hour. Be sure to decide these points:

1. Whether you will have a chairman for each story hour
2. How you will choose your chairman
3. Who will choose the kind of stories for each hour
4. How many stories are to be told each time
5. The time limit for each story

II. You may wish to choose committees to carry out your plans. Decide what committees you will need and who will be on each. Be sure to have a committee to judge how well each one told his story.

The chairman of each committee should list the names of the members and put the list on the bulletin board.

III. When you have finished your discussion, turn to page 15. Judge your discussion by the checks you find there. Decide whether or not you are improving in class discussion.

[ 53 ]

# IS YOUR STORY INTERESTING?

How can you make your story interesting to your audience? Studying a good story and seeing what makes it interesting will help you. Turn to pages 46–49. Review the story and talk over these questions:

I. Does the story open with something happening? Suppose the story had begun this way:

> Once there was a man called Tony Beaver. He had a grandma.

Would you have wished to read the story?

Remember that a good beginning catches the interest of your listeners at once and makes them wish to hear the story.

II. Is there lively conversation in the story? How does it make the story more interesting?

On pages 46–47 read the conversation between Tony and his grandmother. Then read this way of telling the same thing:

> Granny thought Tony was getting thin. She asked him why he did not eat more cakes. Tony said he was not hungry. He wanted to take the rest of the cakes home.

Which do you think is more interesting — the conversation or what you have just read?

III. Does the story have some strange words and expressions in it? How do they add interest to the

[ 54 ]

story?  Which of the words or expressions would you be sure to use if you were to tell the story?

IV. Does the last paragraph of the story make an interesting ending?  Would the story be complete without it?  Does the very last sentence add something to the story?

A good ending for a story is one that keeps up the action and interests the listener.

V. What other things do you like about the way the Tony Beaver story is told?

## RULES FOR STORYTELLING

Make a set of class rules for telling the stories you have read.  You may find some of these helpful.

---

### STANDARDS FOR STORYTELLING

1. Begin with an interesting happening.
2. Make the characters carry on a conversation when you can.
3. Use some of the best words and expressions you found in the story when you read it.
4. Keep the action of the story moving right up to the end.

---

What rules of your own will you add?

Use the rules you list as aids to preparing your own story.  Then, when you listen to the stories of others, use them for judging the stories.

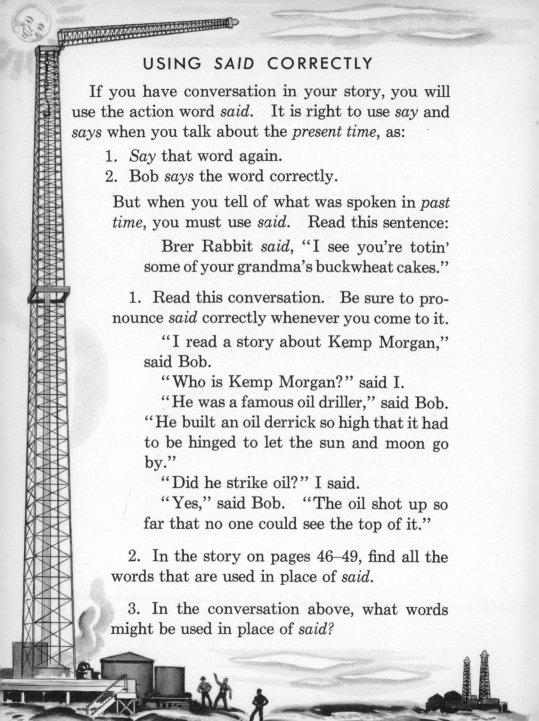

# USING *SAID* CORRECTLY

If you have conversation in your story, you will use the action word *said*. It is right to use *say* and *says* when you talk about the *present time*, as:

1. *Say* that word again.
2. Bob *says* the word correctly.

But when you tell of what was spoken in *past time*, you must use *said*. Read this sentence:

> Brer Rabbit *said*, "I see you're totin' some of your grandma's buckwheat cakes."

1. Read this conversation. Be sure to pronounce *said* correctly whenever you come to it.

> "I read a story about Kemp Morgan," said Bob.
> "Who is Kemp Morgan?" said I.
> "He was a famous oil driller," said Bob. "He built an oil derrick so high that it had to be hinged to let the sun and moon go by."
> "Did he strike oil?" I said.
> "Yes," said Bob. "The oil shot up so far that no one could see the top of it."

2. In the story on pages 46–49, find all the words that are used in place of *said*.

3. In the conversation above, what words might be used in place of *said?*

# OUTLINING YOUR STORY

The story you choose to tell may be a long one. If you are allowed only five minutes to tell your story, you need to decide what to leave out. Read the following suggestions for planning your story:

Make a list of the steps of the story. Think which are the least important and cross them off.

Look over the steps that remain. Think which are the main steps. Then outline them like this:

Tony Beaver and the Buckwheat Cakes

I. Tony's visit to his grandmother

  A. How she baked cakes

  B. How many cakes Tony ate

  C. What he did with the rest

II. Tony's trip home

  A. His meeting with Brer Rabbit

  B. Brer Rabbit's suggestion

  C. How Tony got ahead of Brer Rabbit

Notice that Roman numbers are used for *main topics* and capital letters for *subtopics*. Where are periods used? How does the first word in each topic begin? Give a rule for the capital letters in the title.

[ 57 ]

# BEGAN AND BEGUN

In telling your story, you may wish to use *began* and *begun*.   Read these sentences:

1. Tony *began* to lay his cakes on the log.
2. The Eel River *had begun* to rise.

*Began* does not need a helper.   With *begun*, always use a helping word such as *have*, *has*, or *had*.

1. Read the following sentences aloud, putting in *began* and *begun:*

1. A year ago Joan __?__ to keep a diary.
2. Have the girls __?__ to put their books away?
3. The sun has __?__ to set.
4. When the baby saw his ball, he __?__ to laugh.
5. Ruth __?__ to memorize her favorite poem.
6. Miss Day had __?__ to collect the tests.
7. Just as we were ready to start, the snow __?__ to fall.
8. Jerry __?__ to study his lesson.
9. The river has __?__ to rise very rapidly.
10. As soon as the play was over, the people __?__ to go home.
11. The librarian __?__ to tell us about the books in the library.
12. Had the snow __?__ to melt?

2. Make up three sentences using *began* and three sentences using *begun*.

# EXPLORING YOUR DICTIONARY

In this unit, you have found new words. Make them part of your own vocabulary by learning their meanings.

I. Using the guide words in your dictionary, find each of the following words. Discuss its meaning in class. Give sentences using the word.

exaggerate    shuck (peanuts)    feat    persimmon
ridiculous    spell (word)    griddle    buckwheat

II. Find the word *imagination* in your dictionary. If its meaning is not clear to you, find *imagine* and read its meaning.

If *lumberjack* is not in your dictionary, try *lumberman*, and see whether *lumberjack* is explained there.

In searching for the meaning of a word, do not be easily discouraged. Learn to follow every clue in your dictionary.

III. Your dictionary will also help you understand words and expressions used in dialect.

Find *reckon* and read its dialect meaning.

Find the words *downright* and *puny*. Read their meanings. Then explain the meaning of the expression *downright puny*.

IV. If you have a large dictionary, ask someone to find *tote* in it and read its meaning aloud.

If you do not understand *oil driller*, ask someone to find *oil drill* in the large dictionary and read its meaning. Then explain what an *oil driller* is.

[ 59 ]

# SPEAKING TO AN AUDIENCE

In order to speak distinctly, you must use your lips, teeth, tongue, and throat muscles.

1. Stand before a mirror. Recite a poem and watch your lips. Are you using them as you should, or are you trying to get along without their help?

2. Say the vowels slowly, watching your lips in the mirror: *a   e   i   o   u.*
Say these letters slowly: *t   v   m   s   b   d   f.*
Pronounce these words. Watch your lips, teeth, and tongue.

| rain | reed | ride | road | rude | dog |
|------|------|------|------|------|-----|
| teeth | vote | meat | sit | bite | fat |

3. Answer these questions honestly. If you can say *No* to all of them, you know how to speak before an audience.

1. Do you shift uneasily from one foot to another as you speak before the class?
2. Do you stand with shoulders drooping?
3. Do you move your hands constantly, putting them behind you, in front of you, or in your pockets?
4. Do you gaze at the ceiling or out the window instead of looking into the eyes of your audience?

If you must answer *Yes* to a question, try to correct the fault before you tell your story.

## A RADIO PLAY

One class of girls and boys made up a radio program of American folk tales. Instead of telling a story, a group of children gave it as a radio play.

First of all, the group planned the story in dialogue, to be spoken by the *narrator* (storyteller) and the story characters. They also planned what the *announcer* would say at the beginning and end of the play.

Two of the girls wrote the dialogue. They called it their *radio script*. Jack, who could use the typewriter, made a copy of the script for each person who was to speak over the radio.

You will find their script on the following pages. Perhaps your teacher will ask eight children to take the parts of the persons mentioned in the script, and have them read the dialogue aloud.

[ 61 ]

# TONY BEAVER AND THE WATERMELON

## (*Introduction*)

*Announcer.* Boys and girls of our radio audience, here is our old friend the Narrator, ready to tell you a true story about Tony Beaver's lumber camp in the hills of West Virginia.

*First Boy.* Please tell us about Tony's inventing the lie paper to catch lies.

*First Girl.* No, tell us about the little pet path that Tony sent out to bring strangers to his camp.

*Narrator* (*in the slow, easy drawl of the Southern highlander*). Now, now, children, don't argue. Here's what I'll do. I'll tell you a *new* Tony Beaver story.

*Second Girl.* Oh, that will be wonderful. What is this story about?

*Narrator.* It's about a watermelon. It wasn't the biggest watermelon ever raised in West Virginia, but still it was quite a load for about sixty of Tony's finest oxen.

*Second Boy.* *How* many oxen?

*Narrator.* Only about sixty, but you must understand that these were *very unusual animals.* They could pull several times the weight of that many ordinary oxen.

*Second Girl.* I just can't imagine a watermelon being as big as that.

*Narrator.* Of course you can't. They only grow that big up Eel River near Tony's logging camp.

*First Boy.* Go ahead with the story, Mr. Narrator. I want to hear about the watermelon.

*Narrator.* Tony's lumberjacks had hitched the oxen to the watermelon, and the oxen were slowly dragging the melon to the riverbank. Sawdust Sam and I were standing off at a distance, watching. It happened like this — (*Voice fading*)

(*The Play Begins*)

*Sawdust Sam* (*in a nagging, whining tone*). This is a fool notion of Tony's. He ought to know better than to try to get that watermelon to the river. Something's going to happen.

*Narrator.* But Tony has to do something about that watermelon. It's too big for the lumberjacks to eat, and it's a shame to waste it.

*Sawdust Sam.* He'll never be able to get that watermelon loaded on a raft. He doesn't have a raft big enough, anyhow.

*Narrator.* Oh, Tony can build one bigger than the biggest ship in the world. If he can get the watermelon down the sloping bank to the river's edge, then he can make up his mind how big the raft should be.

*Sawdust Sam.* I can't see how he's going to get it down the bank! It's hard enough to do anything

[ 63 ]

with it on level ground. If it once starts rolling, nothing can stop it — not even Tony.

*Narrator.* Look! The oxen have pulled the melon to the top. I wonder how Tony plans to get it down that steep bank.

*Sawdust Sam.* I'll ask Tony. Here he comes now.

*Tony (in a deep, booming voice).* Good morning, Sam. Hello there, Stranger.

*Narrator.* Hello, Tony.

*Sawdust Sam.* I think you've outreached yourself this time, Tony. I don't see how you're going to get that melon down the riverbank without killing some of the men or the oxen. It's downright dangerous, Tony, just downright dangerous.

*Tony.* Stop your muttering, Sam. Everything's going to be all right.

*Sawdust Sam.* But *how*, Tony, *how?*

*Tony.* Don't you think a crane might do it?

*Sawdust Sam.* None big enough.

*Tony.* The men can *make* a big one.

*Sawdust Sam.* If your foresight was as good as your hindsight, Tony, you wouldn't be in such trouble right now.

*Tony (impatiently).* I'm not in trouble. You're just imagining it. Look! The men have unhitched the oxen and are taking them away! They're going to leave the watermelon on top of the bank until they rig up a crane.

*Sawdust Sam.* That bank doesn't look very secure to me, Tony.

*Tony (slowly).* Maybe you're right this time, Sam. I'd better go — (*shouting*) Watch out, boys! Watch out!

*Narrator (excitedly).* The bank — it's caving in!

*Sawdust Sam.* I told you so! I knew the weight of that watermelon would cave in the bank.

*Tony (shouting).* Stand clear, boys! Get as far away as you can!

*Narrator.* Look at that bank break up! (*Pause*) And there goes the watermelon!

*Sawdust Sam.* Watch that melon roll! It's a good thing the men and the oxen aren't in its path.

(*Sound of heavy splash as the melon hits water*)

*Tony (in an awed tone).* What a splash! I'll bet that will cause a flood down in New Orleans.

*Sawdust Sam.* See! The melon has burst wide open! I knew you'd never get it down-river to market.

*Narrator.* Those pieces of watermelon floating in the river are as big as houses.

*Sawdust Sam.* Why are the men swimming out in the water? It's dangerous! They'd better watch out for those seeds.

*Tony.* Look! They're riding on the seeds!

[ 66 ]

*Narrator (wonderingly).* Well, what do you know about that!

*Sawdust Sam (muttering).* That beats anything I ever saw before.

*Tony.* It's a log jam! That's what it is! Come on, fellows. Let's go help!

*Sawdust Sam.* We can certainly use that lumber.

*Tony (impatiently).* Come on! Hurry, you two! We'll miss all the fun. *(Voice fading out)*

*(Closing)*

*Second Boy.* Do you mean they used those watermelon seeds for *lumber*, Mr. Narrator?

*Narrator.* Why, some of the finest houses in West Virginia were made from those very same watermelon seeds. (*Laughter of children*)

*Announcer.* I am sure that everyone is grateful to the Narrator for giving us the *true* version of that watermelon story. But now, let me tell you about next week. (*Pause*)

Did you ever stop to think about *tomorrow*? We say "Tomorrow, I'll do this," or "Tomorrow, I'll see about that." But *tomorrow* never comes because, when it's time for tomorrow to be here, it's always *today* instead. Well, Tony Beaver found a way to make tomorrow come.

Tune in next week at the same time and hear the *true* story of Tony's tomorrow.

# DISCUSSING THE RADIO PLAY

I. Do you think the dialogue brought out the main points of the play, "Tony Beaver and the Water-melon"? To prove that it did, ask someone to tell the story. See whether he tells all that happened.

II. Into how many parts is the broadcast divided? Who take part in the introduction and the closing? How many characters speak in the play itself?

## A RADIO PROGRAM

For one of your story hours, plan a program of radio plays made from folk tales you have read or told.

I. Divide the class into groups. Let each group choose a story from a list of favorites, plan the dialogue, and decide who shall play each of the characters in the story.

Before the day of the program, each group should practice giving the play until they can do it well enough for others to enjoy.

II. Choose two children to make a microphone. The picture on page 61 may give them some helpful suggestions.

III. Before giving your program, take the lessons on pages 70 and 71. They will help you to speak well.

IV. If you plan to invite another class to hear your radio program, write an invitation. Page 248 will help you to write it correctly.

[ 69 ]

# USING YOUR VOICE WELL

Much of the success of your radio program depends upon how well your plays are planned. But much also depends upon how well each person speaks. A poor voice or two can spoil a good play.

I. At home listen to some good radio programs, especially some in which girls and boys take part. Decide which voices are pleasant to the ear and whether you can hear distinctly all that is said.

Discuss radio voices in class. Make a class list of suggestions about the best kinds of radio voices.

II. In class, read aloud some folk tales you all like. Take turns in the reading, allowing each boy or girl to read a page or so. The rest of the class may listen closely to the voice of the one who is reading. When he is finished, tell him whether or not he is following the suggestions that the class listed.

## CORRECT WORD FORMS

A radio speaker must use correct words. Here is a list of words to remember. Study them carefully. Look out for these little troublemakers.

| Say: | Don't say: | Say: | Don't say: |
|------|-----------|------|-----------|
| ate | "et" | you were | "you was" |
| brought | "brung" | himself | "hisself" |
| burst | "bust" | themselves | "theirselves" |
| isn't ⎫ aren't ⎭ | "ain't" | once | "onct" |
|  |  | across | "acrosst" |

[ 70 ]

# SOUNDING FINAL LETTERS

If you are taking the part of a character who speaks in dialect, you may choose to drop the last letter in some words and say "goin'" for "going" or "eatin'" for "eating." But at other times you must sound the first and final letters of a word clearly if you wish to be heard over the radio.

Here are some words and expressions that people often say carelessly. Practice the forms under *Say* in order to train yourself to speak clearly when you give your radio play.

| *Say:* | *Don't say:* | *Say:* | *Don't say:* |
|--------|--------------|--------|--------------|
| want to | "wanna" | don't you | "doncha" |
| did you | "didja" | going to | "gonna" |
| will you | "willya" | have to | "hafta" |
| kept | "kep" | ought to | "oughta" |
| slept | "slep" | let me | "lemme" |

# SOUNDING VOWELS

Here are more troublemakers. Practice saying them the right way.

Watch the vowels that are underlined.

| *Say:* | *Don't say:* | *Say:* | *Don't say:* |
|--------|--------------|--------|--------------|
| catch | "ketch" | men | "min" |
| touch | "tetch" | any | "inny" |
| get | "git" | just | "jist" |
| can | "kin" | or | "er" |

# AN ORIGINAL TALL TALE

Near Nancy's home there is a deep stream called Bottomless River. Nancy made up a tale about it. Read it and decide whether you like it.

## MOOKA AND THE BOTTOMLESS RIVER

Long ago, even before the time of the Red Man, there lived in North America a race of giants. Their king was named Mooka, and he was taller and stronger than all the others. He was a Super-Giant.

At first Mooka was a good king. But soon he became wicked and cruel. He made the people slave all the time. He made them build the Rocky Mountains so that he could play leapfrog over them. He had the giants make Niagara Falls so that he could use it for a shower bath.

Finally he ordered the slaves to dig out a river so deep that it would be deeper than the ocean itself, as he wanted to be able to take a bath in it standing up.

The slave giants did as they were told. They dug a river that they thought was deep enough. It took them hundreds of years.

As Mooka stepped into the water, the slaves trembled with fear. What if they had not made the river deep enough!

But nothing at all happened. Mooka just disappeared.

The giants waited and waited, but Mooka did not come back. They swam up and down the river to see what had happened to him.

Suddenly they understood! Mooka's weight had broken through the thin layer of earth that separated their river from another river on the other side of the world. Very likely he set up a kingdom in China, or wherever it was that he came out.

The giants did not know what to do without their leader. In time they all died. All that is left to prove that this story is true is Bottomless River.

I. Do you think Nancy made up a good tale? What do you like about it? What don't you like?

II. What could Nancy have done to improve her tale about Bottomless River?

## Check Test 4: Correct Words

Write these sentences. Put in the correct word.

1. (Is, Are) you ready to go to the library?
2. Bob and Jerry (isn't, aren't) ready yet.
3. We (was, were) going tomorrow.
4. Who (is, are) your favorite folk-tale hero?
5. Stormalong (was, were) my hero until I read about Mike Fink.
6. (Isn't, Aren't) you and Joe writing a story?
7. I am working on a tall tale, but Joe (isn't, aren't).
8. I hope the library (isn't, aren't) closed.
9. It (wasn't, weren't) closed last week.
10. (Wasn't, Weren't) you there yesterday?

If you make mistakes, turn to page 281 for help.

# MAKING UP YOUR OWN TALE

I. Try making up a tale of your own. Is there some natural object in your state or community that has always seemed strange or mysterious to you? Is it a cliff, a cave, a deep pool, or a dark forest? Have you heard a folk tale about it already?

For example, many tales have been told about the Old Man of the Mountain, which can be seen in the White Mountains of New Hampshire. Perhaps you have heard some of the strange tales told by early trappers about the wonders of Yellowstone National Park or the Grand Canyon of the Colorado.

Here are other suggestions that may help you in planning your tale:

1. Your tale may be about a giant like Paul Bunyan or Tony Beaver. It is told that Paul Bunyan scooped out the Great Lakes to give Babe, his blue ox, a place to drink. Make up a similar tale about an imaginary hero whom you admire.

2. You might prefer to write an Indian tale in which the Great Spirit causes a large cave to appear for some reason. As a punishment or a reward, he may turn someone into a hill of an unusual shape, such as a crouching cougar, or a buffalo's hump, or a man's head.

3. If you wish, write about some strange little creatures who play pranks on people. You probably know that fliers have made up tales about naughty

little fellows, called gremlins, who do harm to the engine and other airplane parts. Think of a name to give your little folk.

II. When you are ready, plan for a class campfire. Pretend that you are all sitting about a campfire. Tell your original tales.

After the storytelling, vote to decide which original tale was the best. Then discuss the tale and try to decide why you liked it.

# A BOOK OF ORIGINAL TALES

Would you like to make a book of your original tales? If you would, follow these suggestions:

I. Discuss (*a*) the kind and size of paper to use for your stories, (*b*) how to make the cover, (*c*) the date when the stories must be finished.

II. Choose a committee for making the cover. Choose a committee of editors to check the stories, and a third committee to put the book together and to make the title page and table of contents. Put the book in your library so that all may read it.

III. Make a set of rules for writing the tales. Be sure to include the ones listed below:

1. Plan the top margin wider than the side margins and the bottom margin wider than the top.
2. Choose an interesting title. Leave extra space below the title.
3. Have at least one paragraph for each topic in your outline. Indent the first word of each paragraph.
4. Do not string sentences together with *and's*. Use capital letters and punctuation to keep sentences apart.
5. Draw or paint a picture of the most interesting event in the story.
6. Edit your tale carefully when you have completed it.

# UNDERSTANDING SENTENCES

If you want your story to be good, you need to be very sure that you know how to build good sentences. The lessons on pages 77–85 will help you to understand better how to build them.

Your teacher will read to you the following paragraphs from another folk tale by Carl Carmer. Close your eyes. See whether you can tell when she has read a complete thought. Listen to hear each separate sentence.

### The White Mustang

The Ghost Horse of the Prairies was first discovered by some of our Western Indians. Their keen eyes spied him, far in the distance, speeding across the level stretch of the prairies. Swift-footed and graceful he was, and not even their greatest hunters could ever keep pace with him. Always he outran them, vanishing in the haze of a distant horizon.

*(How many sentences have you heard?)*

Even today every cowboy dreams of catching the White Mustang. What a feat it would be to tame

him and ride him at a great rodeo!  Cowboys who
have chased him say that he is the most beautiful
animal in the world.  He is also the fastest.  Though
he has been chased by clever riders, he has never yet
been forced into a gallop.  In a beautiful rocking pace
he measures off mile after mile, leaving his pursuers
far behind.

*(How many sentences?)*

Many folks claim that the White Mustang is not
real flesh and blood.  They say that he will never
grow old.  Rifle bullets pass right through him without hurting him or slowing down his speed.  No
matter how far he is pursued, he never tires.

*(How many sentences?)*

I.  Did you all hear the same number of sentences,
or complete thoughts, in each of the three paragraphs?
Skim through each paragraph.  Count the sentences.
Were you correct?  If you were, you can tell when a
speaker has expressed a complete thought.

II.  Look over the paragraphs again.  Which sentence is the shortest? the longest?  Is the thought
expressed by the shortest as complete as that expressed by the longest?

III.  Your teacher will read you some paragraphs
from a story in your reader.  Listen closely and count
the complete thoughts as she reads.  Check your-
selves by finding the paragraphs and counting the
sentences.

[ 78 ]

Remember these facts:

*A sentence expresses a complete thought.* Any group of words that expresses a complete thought is a sentence. Any group of words that does not express a complete thought is not a sentence.

## Practice in Recognizing Sentences

1. Read this paragraph and watch for each complete thought. Then write the paragraph, using capital letters and punctuation marks correctly.

Midas had more gold than any other king in the world even then he was not satisfied he wished that the palace furniture were made of gold he wished that the roses in his garden would turn to gold Midas felt that he could never be happy until everything he touched turned to shining gold.

2. In this paragraph some of the sentences have been cut apart. Read the paragraph and find the mistakes. Then write the paragraph correctly.

His wish came true. The bedcovers had turned to gold. When he waked in the morning. His clothing became heavy and stiff and yellow. As he dressed himself. The beautiful flowers in his garden turned to gold. As he touched them. He kissed his little daughter. Midas was brokenhearted. When she changed into a golden statue.

[ 79 ]

# FINDING SENTENCE PARTS

Every sentence needs two parts. One part names something, and the other part tells about what was named. Notice the sentence parts in these well-known sentences:

| The Part That Names | The Part That Tells |
|---|---|
| 1. Little Miss Muffet | sat on a tuffet. |
| 2. The mouse | ran up the clock. |
| 3. Simple Simon | met a pieman. |
| 4. Little Robin Redbreast | sat upon a rail. |
| 5. I | had a little pony. |
| 6. His name | was Dapple Gray. |

In which sentence is the first part a single word? *I* is used in place of the name of the person speaking.

Here are some more sentences from nursery rhymes. See whether you can divide each one into the part that names something and the part that tells about it.

1. Old King Cole was a merry old soul.
2. He called for his fiddlers three.
3. Little Bo-Peep has lost her sheep.
4. The king was in his countinghouse.
5. The queen was in the parlor.
6. She was eating bread and honey.
7. Humpty Dumpty sat on a wall.
8. The cow jumped over the moon.

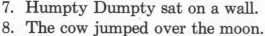

[ 80 ]

## Practice with Sentences

1. Here are some familiar sentences that are cut into two parts. In column 1 are the parts that name something. For each naming part in column 1, find the right telling part in column 2. Then write the sentence. Be sure to begin and end it correctly.

|               1               |               2               |
|-------------------------------|-------------------------------|
| 1. Jack                       | fell fast asleep.             |
| 2. Little Bo-Peep             | had a great fall.             |
| 3. Old Mother Hubbard         | is in the well.               |
| 4. Humpty Dumpty              | sat in a corner.              |
| 5. Little Jack Horner         | jumped over the candlestick.  |
| 6. Pussy                      | went to the cupboard.         |

2. Write the following sentences. In each one, draw a line between the part that names something and the part that tells about it, like this:

The White Mustang | was a ghost horse.
The cowboys of today | dream of catching him.

1. Some Western Indians discovered the White Mustang.
2. He is not an animal of flesh and blood.
3. A rifle bullet passes right through him.
4. It does not slow his speed.
5. The best riders pursued the White Mustang.

3. Write two sentences of your own about the White Mustang. Draw a line between the part that names and the part that tells.

[ 81 ]

# COMBINING SHORT SENTENCES

Sometimes it is necessary to use a short sentence. But a paragraph or a story made up entirely of short sentences is likely to be tiresome.

Read this paragraph aloud. Notice how short the sentences are. Notice, too, that most of them begin with the word *He*.

> Pecos Bill saw the cyclone advancing toward him. He leaped upon his horse. He rode to meet the twister. He twirled his lasso into position. He threw the rope with remarkable speed and accuracy. He was able to lasso the monster.

See how *when* may be used to join the first two sentences in the paragraph:

> *When* Pecos Bill saw the cyclone advancing toward him, he leaped upon his horse.

Try to join the third and fourth sentences by using *as*. Show how to join the fifth and sixth sentences by using *because*.

Read the following paragraph. Why is it more interesting than the paragraph above? Notice, too, that the sentences begin in different ways.

> When Pecos Bill saw the cyclone advancing toward him, he leaped upon his horse. As he rode to meet the twister, he twirled his lasso into position. He was able

to lasso the monster because he threw the rope with remarkable speed and accuracy.

When the part that begins with a connecting word comes first in the sentence, place a comma after it, as you see in the first and second sentences of the paragraph. There is no comma in the third sentence because the part that begins with the connecting word does not come first.

### Practice with Sentences

Combine each pair of short sentences below. You may have to change some words around or drop others. Use the connecting word in parentheses before the number. Write the longer sentence correctly.

(while)    1. You watch the fire. I will hunt for more wood.

(if)       2. You can use a telescope. Then you can see more stars.

(for)      3. Mary and I went early. We were quite weary.

(after)    4. The chipmunk had filled his cheeks with nuts. He ran to his nest.

(when)     5. The leader will clap his hands. Then both teams must start.

(because)  6. James brought the book back. He had finished it.

(where)    7. Put this box on the shelf. There is more room on it.

(since)    8. I haven't seen Bob. He went away last week.

# WRITING COMPLETE SENTENCES

When Agnes checked the tale she had written, she found she had cut off part of a sentence. This is what she had written:

After the giant had pulled up an oak tree by the roots. He whacked off the branches and used the tree for a walking stick.

How can you tell that "After the giant had pulled up an oak tree by the roots" is not a sentence?

When you join two short sentences, remember that the part that begins with *if, after, when, because, before,* or one of the other connecting words is not a complete thought. Do not write it as a sentence.

I. Read this paragraph. See whether you can find parts of sentences that are cut off from the sentences to which they belong. Read aloud the parts that are not sentences.

Paul Bunyan's blue ox was not always blue in color. When Babe was a little calf. He was snow-white. Then came the winter of the blue snow. The ox turned a sky-blue color. After he had stood out in the snow for six days.

Tell how you would correct the paragraph.

II. On the next page is another paragraph that is carelessly written. As you read it aloud, you will find periods that tell you to drop your voice where you should not drop it. That shows you that parts of sentences have been cut off from the sentences to which they belong. Read the paragraphs correctly. Then tell how to correct them.

Paul Bunyan's blue ox was the biggest ox in the world. It was impossible to know how much he weighed. Because there were no scales big enough to weigh him. When Paul was standing near Babe's front feet. He had to use field glasses to see what the ox's hind feet were doing.

One time a jay bird started to fly from one of Babe's horns to the other. If he had known how far it was. He would not have tried it. He started in the middle of winter. Spring had arrived. Long before he reached his destination.

# WRITING CONVERSATION

Beth said that Nancy's story on pages 72–73 would have been better if some part of it had been written as a conversation. Do you agree with Beth?

If you use conversation in your story, you must know how to write it. Read this bit of conversation from a tale that Warren wrote.

"Who are you?" asked Crop Ear.
Chuck replied, "My name is Bob Hunt, but the boys call me Chuck."
"I am a coyote," Crop Ear explained.
Chuck laughed, "What a joke!"

I. In this conversation, how many persons spoke? How many times did each one speak? Did you notice that each speech started a new paragraph?

II. The exact words of a speaker are a *quotation*. Look at the *quotation marks* before and after the quotation in each sentence.

III. Notice that the first word in each quotation begins with a capital letter.

IV. In the first sentence, why does a question mark follow the quotation? Why is there an exclamation mark after the quotation in the last sentence?

When the quotation does not require a question mark or an exclamation point, use a comma to separate the quotation from the rest of the sentence, as in the third sentence.

In the second and fourth sentences, where is the comma placed? There must always be some mark of punctuation between the quotation and the rest of the sentence.

Use these standards for writing conversation.

---

### HOW TO WRITE CONVERSATION

1. Start a new paragraph for each speech.
2. Begin the first word in the quotation with a capital letter.
3. Place quotation marks before and after each quotation.
4. Separate the quotation from the rest of the sentence by some mark of punctuation.

---

### *Practice with Conversation*

Copy the following conversation. Put in quotation marks where they are needed.

Where is Mooka?   questioned the giants.

Perhaps he has drowned,   said a very young giant.

The old giant exclaimed,   Our king cannot drown.

Then where is he?   the youngest one asked.

I think I know,   said the old giant.

[ 87 ]

# HOW WELL
# DO YOU REMEMBER?

Take these tests to find out how well you remember what you learned in Unit Two. If you make a mistake in any test, turn to pages 90–91 and take the practice having the same Roman number as the test.

TEST I. Write each sentence. Put in *says* or *said*.

1. "This book I am reading __?__ that Davy Crockett was a real person," __?__ Bob.
2. "Miss Grant told us that," __?__ Henry.
3. "She also __?__ that Davy Crockett was a famous Indian Scout," __?__ Henry.
4. "I didn't know she __?__ that," Bob replied.

TEST II. Write this outline correctly. Put in numbers and capital letters.

the story of Hiawatha
who his family were
his grandmother
his father
how he lived
in his childhood
when he became a man

TEST III. Write each sentence. Use *began* or *begun*.

1. Bob sat down and __?__ to read his new book.
2. Henry has __?__ a new book of Irish fairy tales.
3. Yesterday I __?__ to study for the test.
4. Have you __?__ to study for the test?

[ 88 ]

TEST IV. Write each sentence. Draw a line between the part that names something and the part that tells about it.

1. Tony was carrying some buckwheat cakes.
2. The persimmons belonged to Brer Rabbit.
3. Tony was willing to share the cakes.
4. Brer Rabbit yelled, "Bingo!"

TEST V. Combine each pair of short sentences to make a long sentence. Use good connecting words. Place the comma where necessary.

1. This is the house.   Jack built it.
2. You build the fire.   I will unpack the lunch.
3. You haven't an umbrella.   I will leave mine.
4. Tom found the book on the shelf.   Anne had put it there.

TEST VI. In each sentence find the quotation. Then write the sentence and put in quotation marks.

1. What is that, Nokomis?   asked Hiawatha.
2. That is the owl and owlet speaking in their native language,   answered Nokomis.
3. Do not shoot me,   begged the rabbit.

# IF YOU NEED HELP

PRACTICE I.   A.  On page 56, review *says* and *said*.

B.  Write each sentence, using *says* or *said:*

1. Last month Henry __?__ that Bob could not skate.
2. Now he __?__ that Bob is a good skater.
3. Joe __?__ "This newspaper __?__ that there is to be a skating contest next month."
4. "That will be a lot of fun," __?__ Nancy.

PRACTICE II.   A.  Review the lesson on page 57.

B.  Write the following outline.  Be sure to use numbers and letters correctly.

> The Work of the School Librarian

> Taking care of the books
> > Keeping them in order
> > Checking them in and out
> Helping the boys and girls
> > Locating materials for study
> > Selecting books to read for pleasure

PRACTICE III.   A.  Review the lesson *began* and *begun* on page 58.

B.  Write these sentences, using *began* and *begun:*

1. The boys __?__ to laugh when they saw Bob's face.
2. Have the girls __?__ to get ready?
3. Miss Graham has __?__ to read the story.
4. The girls __?__ to clap their hands.

PRACTICE IV. *A.* Review the lesson on page 80.

*B.* Copy each sentence and then draw a line between the two parts:

1. I like to read books of fairy tales.
2. The boys read many Indian stories.
3. Our class likes American folk tales.
4. The librarian has ordered some new books of folk tales.

PRACTICE V. *A.* Read the lesson on pages 82–83.

*B.* Make long sentences out of the pairs of short sentences, using these connecting words: (1) *as,* (2) *since,* (3) *when,* (4) *where.*

1. Miss Smith was reading the last line. The bell rang.
2. Doris could not go. Nancy stayed with her.
3. You will hear the gong. It will be two o'clock.
4. Here is the book. Bob left it here.

PRACTICE VI. *A.* Review the use of quotation marks on pages 86–87.

*B.* Write these sentences, putting in quotation marks where they are needed:

1. Where is Doris? asked Miss Poole.
2. I saw her in the library, Jerry said.
3. She was looking for the book *Heidi,* Henry explained.
4. Here she is now! broke in Nancy.

[ 91 ]

# Unit Three

## CONVERSATION

### TALKING ABOUT HOBBIES

Often Miss Dean's class had a conversation period in which they talked about topics that were of interest to them. They learned that conversation is a way of having an enjoyable time. They also discovered that their conversations were helping them to know one another better. That is, they were becoming better friends and fellow workers.

Early in the year the class spent one conversation period in talking about the hobbies they had begun during the past summer. Perhaps you will enjoy reading this part of their conversation:

*Margaret.* Rose has the most wonderful dolls.

*Bob (questioningly).* Dolls? I thought girls of Rose's age were too old to play with dolls.

*Sue (explaining).* Oh, but Rose's dolls aren't just playthings. Dolls are Rose's hobby.

[ 93 ]

*Frank.* How can dolls be a hobby? I don't know anyone who makes a collection of dolls.

*Anne (laughing).* Then we'd better introduce you to Rose, Frank. Rose has a collection of dolls that could teach you a thing or two.

*Frank (protesting).* Oh, of course I know Rose. But what I don't know is Rose's collection. Please tell us about it, Rose. There must be other people here who don't know about your dolls.

*Rose (explaining).* My dolls represent the people of fairy tales. I choose one of my favorite stories, and then look for the story in different books to see how the characters are pictured. Next, I make the dolls represent the characters. Making the costumes and dressing the dolls are the most interesting parts of the whole job.

*Jean.* How many sets of characters have you, Rose, and where do you keep them?

*Rose.* I have characters for seven stories. I keep the dolls in a cabinet in my room. The cabinet has glass doors. Every time I come into my room, it is fun to see my favorite story characters looking at me.

*Frank.* You win, Rose. You certainly have a hobby that is fun. And I can see that it takes a lot of work and skill to make those doll characters. I agree that your hobby is as good as mine.

*Rose.* What is your hobby, Frank?

*Frank.* Making airplane models.

*Arthur.* You ought to see Frank's models. He made six new ones this summer. That makes a total of seventeen planes.

*Ted.* Doesn't it take a lot of money to keep up with your hobby, Frank? I know you have to pay a

good price for a set of parts for a model plane. Some cost as much as four or five dollars.

*Frank* (*explaining*). But I don't buy sets of parts. In the model magazine that I read, there are patterns for each part. I copy the patterns and make the parts myself.

*Herbert.* Then where do you get your materials?

*Frank.* A good bit is odd material that I have picked up myself, like pieces of tin, metal, wire, and tubing. But I do have to buy the balsa wood. It's strange, though, to see how much you can find when you are on the lookout for materials.

*Jimmy.* I'm glad to hear about your models, Frank. I've been collecting airplane pictures, but I think I'll try my hand at models myself. Pictures seem tame beside them.

*June.* This summer I took up weaving. Down at the Vacation School there was a class in weaving that I attended. Mother gave me a loom for my birthday. It's fun to make interesting patterns with yarns of different colors.

*Fred.* What kinds of things do you weave?

*June.* On the small loom at the school, I made holders to use in the kitchen. On my own loom, I can weave a piece eight by ten inches. By sewing six pieces together, I made a mat for the table in my room.

*Agnes (exclaiming).* How interesting your hobby sounds! I never thought of weaving except among the Indians or in a factory.

*Beth.* Oh, a great many persons take up weaving as an art. Mother has a friend who has a very large loom. She can weave cloth for dresses and suits. Hand-woven cloth sells for a high price.

*Joe.* My father's hobby is making ship models. By watching him, I became interested in his hobby. I think I will take it up myself.

*Tim.* I know a boy who collects matchbook covers.

*Allan.* That kind of hobby doesn't get you anywhere. You soon get tired of it, and it doesn't teach you anything. If you collect coins, you learn a lot of interesting things about other countries and their history.

*Grace.* Why don't you tell us about your hobby, Billy?

*Arthur.* I guess he hasn't had a chance. Shall we give Billy the floor? He's a camera expert.

*All (in unison).* Yes, yes.

*Billy.* I began taking pictures with a little camera I got for Christmas when I was seven years old. Now I have a kodak with a fast lens. Father is a photographer on a newspaper, and he has taught me all I know about taking pictures. But experience has taught me some things, too. There's a lot more to photography than just taking a shot. You have to know what to choose for a good shot, and also how to develop the film and make interesting prints.

*Arthur.* You might as well know that Billy's a famous photographer. He won a first prize in the last exhibition at the Art Museum.

I. What makes you think that the class enjoyed their conversation about hobbies? Why do you think they enjoyed it?

II. How many girls and boys took part in the conversation? How did that help to add to the interest of the conversation period?

III. Find and read some good questions that helped to keep the conversation going.

IV. Tell which speakers were successful in drawing others into the conversation.

V. Find instances to show that good conversation may give interesting information or new ideas to those taking part in it.

## WHAT TO TALK ABOUT

You have probably been with a group when no one present seemed to say anything that you cared to listen to, or when no one could think of anything to say. Such an experience is always a painful one, and you find yourself wishing that you were reading a good book, or out fishing, or working on your hobby.

What is a good topic for conversation? First of all, it must be a topic that will interest everyone or almost everyone in the group. Talk over the topics you might enjoy. You might think of hobbies first, since most girls and boys have hobbies. You might also think of books you have enjoyed, school sports or athletics, or trips you have taken.

I. Make a list of conversation topics that would interest your group. Keep the list for future use.

II. Tell why the following topics may be of little interest to your hearers:

A new dress or suit you have been given
A quarrel you had with a brother or sister
Why you do not like spinach
What you think of John Doe
Why you do not like arithmetic
How tired you feel

Perhaps you may decide that it is possible to talk about personal matters such as these to a very close friend. But you may bore even a close friend with complaints and criticisms.

III. Plan to have a class conversation period once a week. Decide in advance what the topic for each period will be. Use topics from the list you have made for exercise I.

IV. Later, make a list of topics about things you ought to be interested in, such as the following:

How we might improve our school
The advantages of our town or community
Improvements we would like to see in our community
What our public library offers us

After you decide the topic for the next conversation period, each girl and boy should think over the topic and prepare something to say.

# "KEEPING THE BALL IN PLAY"

A good conversation is like a game in which the players toss the ball from one to the other. When the ball drops to the ground or goes out-of-bounds, the game lags.

As a member of a group, you have a responsibility for keeping the conversation going. Sometimes your responsibility lies in catching the ball and tossing it on; that is, you must take up the point someone has just made, add your remarks, or raise a question. You should do it in such an interesting way that someone else thinks of something to say. Much of the time your responsibility consists of listening closely to what each speaker says in order to get a cue for something to say. When you do that, you are "keeping your eye on the ball."

In your conversation periods, try to follow these suggestions:

1. If possible, sit in a group so that you may all face one another.

2. Do not raise your hands, or stand to speak. If you watch the speaker, you will know when you may speak.

3. Speak to the whole group, not to one person.

4. Speak clearly enough for all to hear.

5. Remember that a question is a good way "to keep the ball in play."

6. Stay on the topic, or you will toss the conversational ball out-of-bounds.

# COURTESIES IN CONVERSATION

In a conversation, each member of the group must respect the rights of all the others.

Tell why the following are acts of discourtesy in a conversation:

A heated argument between two people
Unkind criticism of a speaker
Too many speeches by one person
Interrupting a speaker

When it is necessary to correct a speaker's error, there is a courteous way to do it. You may say,

I'm sorry, Anne, but you made a slight mistake. The Story Hour at the library is at 3:00 o'clock, not 3:30.

If two persons should happen to start speaking at the same time, one may say,

I'm sorry, Tom. I'll wait until you have finished.

If you wish to disagree with someone, it is courteous to say,

I'm sorry to disagree with you, Ellen, but I don't think that the playground director is too strict. He has to see that the rules are obeyed so that every boy and girl may have their rights.

Remember to practice courtesies of this kind when you have your conversation periods.

# USING CORRECT WORDS

You have probably learned that an untidy and incorrect letter is a discourtesy to the one who is to receive it. Just so, careless use of words is a discourtesy to your listeners. In your conversations, use the correct forms you have learned. This test will show you how well you remember some of them.

## Check Test 5: Correct Words

Write these sentences. Use the correct word.

1. Jane has (wrote, written) some clever poems.
2. Joe (wrote, written) a fine story for our class magazine.
3. You (may, can) have my fudge recipe.
4. Bob and (I, me) work together on our stamp collections.
5. Alice can paint very (well, good).
6. Tom says he has never (ate, eaten) better doughnuts than mine.
7. He (ate, et) six this morning.
8. Father hasn't (any, no) camera.
9. We didn't see (any, no) strange birds on that trip.
10. There weren't (any, no) eggs in the bluebird's nest.

If you make a mistake on this test, turn to pages 281–282 for help.

# USING THE CORRECT VERB

In many sentences you speak or write, you use action words, such as *grow, blow, fly,* or *throw.* Such action words are called *verbs.*

Most verbs have more than one form.

| Present Time | Past Time | With a Helper |
|---|---|---|
| grow | grew | has grown |
| throw | threw | have thrown |
| blow | blew | had blown |
| fly | flew | were flown |

Notice that not one of these four verbs has a form that ends in *ed.* It is wrong to say "growed," "throwed," or "blowed."

It is never correct to use a helping verb such as *has, have,* or *had* with the forms listed under *Past Time.* Helping verbs may be used with the forms in the right-hand column.

Write each of the following sentences, putting in the correct word. Look at the lists above for help in choosing the correct form.

### *Flew* or *Flown?*

1. Have you ever __?__ a model airplane?
2. Ten planes __?__ in the race.
3. Jerry had never __?__ a model plane before.
4. Jack's plane __?__ higher than Jerry's.
5. It __?__ high in the air.

### Grew or Grown?

1. The kittens have __?__ large enough to climb out of their basket.
2. Has the black kitten __?__ larger than the others?
3. No, the yellow kitten __?__ faster than the black one.
4. The gray kitten's fur has __?__ much longer.

### Blew or Blown?

1. The wind __?__ hard all night long.
2. Our boat was __?__ far out to sea.
3. Has the foghorn __?__ this morning?
4. The wind __?__ our tent down.
5. The boat whistle __?__ shrilly.

### Threw or Thrown?

1. As Jack __?__ the horseshoe, he lost his balance.
2. Has Jerry ever __?__ any ringers?
3. Ben __?__ a ringer yesterday.
4. Several of the boys have __?__ them.

# IMPROVING YOUR CONVERSATION

As you continue your conversation periods, you will be interested to learn whether your class is improving in the art of conversation. Here are some standards by which you may judge your progress.

STANDARDS FOR CONVERSATION
1. Was the topic interesting to most of the group?
2. Did all or most of the group take part?
3. Did each speaker help to keep the conversation going?
4. Were there good questions?
5. Was the language of the group correct?

Use the following questions to check your part in a conversation. You may ask your classmates to help you answer some of them.

1. Did I do my part to keep the conversation going?
2. Did I talk too often or too long?
3. Did I tell what was of interest to others?
4. Did I ask good questions?
5. Was my language correct?
6. Was my voice pleasant to hear and loud enough to reach everyone?
7. Did I practice courtesy?

Can you think of other questions with which to check your conversation?

# OVERWORKED WORDS

Read the following sentences that were used in a conversation. Look for overworked words that could easily be replaced by words that express more clearly what you mean.

1. That was a swell party!
2. Wasn't yesterday a grand day for a lawn party?
3. I had a swell time.
4. Didn't Jane look nice?
5. I had an awful time getting there.
6. The cookies were awfully good, weren't they?

Do you use such words as "swell," "grand," "nice," "awful," "awfully"? These words are used so often and for so many purposes that they have become almost meaningless; that is, they really do not give a clear idea to the listener.

I. For each sentence above, think of a better word to use in place of the overworked word. Then give the sentence aloud. For sentence 1, you might say,

That was a *delightful* party.
That was an *unusual* party.
That was an *enjoyable* party.

II. List some of the overworked words and expressions that you hear about you every day. Then think of more interesting words to use in place of them. Try to use these words in your everyday conversation.

# TABLE CONVERSATION

As you improve in conversation, practice what you learn in your table conversation at home. The evening meal is often the only time you see all of your family together. Do your part to make the dinner-table conversation interesting.

In the first place, always choose a good topic for table conversation. Do not discuss unpleasant things or happenings.

Decide which of the following topics are not suited for mealtime conversation:

How the dentist hurt you
A book you have just read
A new movie
How bad the weather is
Your success with your hobby
An important event that you read about
    in the newspaper
Your sick pet
A good joke
How well your garden is growing
A fight you saw

Next, practice table courtesies. Of course, you will remember the conversation courtesies you have learned. Besides these, remember that there are courtesies about asking for and receiving food.

From each pair of sentences on the opposite page, choose the one which you consider the more courteous.

1. { Please pass me the butter, Tom.
   { Shove the butter down this way.

2. { Take it away.  I don't want any more.
   { I've had enough cereal, thank you.

3. { Please excuse me.  I don't want to be late
       for school.
   { I've got to go.

Lastly, avoid unpleasant scenes and unnecessary activities at the table.  Discuss the following:

Criticizing someone at the table
Playing tricks with your table tools
Criticizing the food
Complaining because someone else got a bigger
    piece than you did

[ 109 ]

## ANSWERING A QUESTION

Many times during the day, you may be asked a question. Are you always courteous and thoughtful when you give your answer? Or do you sometimes give a hasty and careless reply?

Read this conversation:

*Stranger* (*to a boy passing*). Is there a mailbox in this neighborhood?

*Mark.* No, there isn't. But the post office is only a block and a half away. Just walk on down to the end of this block, turn left, and walk a half block. You will be right at the post office.

If Mark had answered only *No* to the stranger's question, he would have made the man ask a second question, such as, "Where can I find a mailbox?" Mark was thoughtful enough to think what help the man needed. So he gave him a complete answer that would supply the facts he needed.

It is always well to put yourself in the place of the questioner and think what help he needs. Then it is possible to give a helpful answer.

I. Read the following questions and answers. In each case tell which answer is the more courteous and helpful one. Try to give good reasons for your choice.

1. *Principal.* Is this gymnasium day for your class?
   *Bob.* No.
   *Jim.* No, Mr. Taylor. Our day is Friday.

2. *Mother.* Are you ready for school?
   *Anne.* No.
   *Sue.* No, Mother. But I will be when I find a handkerchief.

II. Tell why the following are discourteous or thoughtless answers in many instances:

Nodding your head to mean *yes* or *no*

Shrugging your shoulders instead of speaking your reply

Answering without looking at the person asking the question

Saying, "Uh-huh."

[ 111 ]

# GREETINGS AND GOOD-BYS

When you meet a close friend about your own age, you use any greeting that seems right to you. You may say, "Hello, Jane," or "Hello there, Tom," or "Hi, Jim."

But when you come to school each morning and meet an older person such as your teacher, principal, or school nurse, a more dignified greeting is in good form. When you meet friends of your parents, you also should use such a greeting. Here are some greetings that are courteous:

Good morning, Miss Wilson.
Good afternoon, Mrs. Nelson.
How do you do, Mr. Craig?
Good evening, Dr. Jones.

You may follow the same practices in saying good-by. To a close friend of your own age you will say, "So long, Tom," "See you later, Betty," or any other good-by that you may choose.

But to an older person, it is courteous and correct to say:

Good-by, Mr. Adams.
Good night, Father.

As you meet and greet people at school or on the street, remember to use the courteous and correct greetings for those who are older than yourself.

Sometimes you go to a party at the home of a friend. When you arrive at the house, remember to greet the mother and father of your friend, using one of the greetings you have just read.

When you are ready to leave the party, find your friend's parents, if both are present, and say good-by to them as well as to your friend. In addition to the farewell, be sure to express your thanks and appreciation for the good time you have had.

Tell whether you think the following are correct:

*Bob.* Good night, Mrs. James. Thank you for a very good time.

*Sue.* Thank you for a very fine time, Bill. I thought the games were great fun. Good-by.

## CARRYING
## A MESSAGE

"Jack, will you please take a message to the principal's office?" asked the teacher.

"Certainly, Miss Dean," replied Jack.

"Please tell Mr. West that I shall stay after school for play practice tomorrow afternoon instead of this afternoon. Wait a minute! Don't go yet!" she exclaimed as Jack edged toward the door.

"Ask him to put the notice on the bulletin board in the hall so that the boys and girls in the play will not stay tonight," she added.

Jack rushed to the principal's office.

"Mr. West, Miss Dean told me to tell you something," Jack said as he entered the office.

"Wait, Jack, until I finish this telephone conversation," Mr. West said.

After he had hung the receiver back on the hook, Mr. West turned to the boy.

"Well, Jack, what is it?" he asked.

"It's about — it's something about practicing for the play," said Jack. "Miss Dean said — uh — something about staying after school," he added. He was having a hard time remembering just what Miss Dean had said.

"I'm glad she reminded me of that," said Mr. West. "I'll put an announcement on the bulletin board right away to remind the boys and girls in the play to stay after school this afternoon. Thank you for the message."

"Yes, sir," answered Jack, much relieved.

"What did Mr. West say?" asked Miss Dean when Jack came back.

"He said he would put the notice on the bulletin board," replied Jack.

What do you think happened after school?

I. Have someone read aloud the account of Jack's carrying the message to the principal. Tell what mistakes Jack made at each step.

II. Choose a girl to take the part of the teacher, a boy to be the principal, and another boy to take the part of Jack. Ask them to act a scene like that described in the story, but to carry it through as though the message had been delivered correctly.

After they have finished, the class may give suggestions for improving the scene.

III. Make a list of suggestions for receiving and delivering a message.

IV. Act other scenes showing how to deliver a message correctly. Your teacher will choose someone to deliver a message and someone to receive it. The class may judge how well they follow the suggestions that were listed.

# RECEIVING A CALLER

Patty Hill was a member of the hospitality committee in Miss Dean's class. One day during the week, when it was Patty's turn to receive guests, a visitor came to the door. Read the conversation that took place:

*Visitor.* Good morning. I am Ellen Lane's mother. May I visit your class this morning?

*Patty.* Good morning, Mrs. Lane. I am Patty Hill. Please come in. I am sure Miss Dean will be glad to see you.

*Visitor.* Thank you, Patty.

*Patty* (*addressing teacher*). Miss Dean, this is Mrs. Lane, Ellen's mother. She has come to visit us. Mrs. Lane, this is Miss Dean.

*Miss Dean.* How do you do, Mrs. Lane. We are very glad to see you. Patty will take care of you.

Patty took Mrs. Lane's coat, led her to a seat, and explained to her what the class was doing.

I. Did you like the manner in which Patty greeted the visitor and made the introductions?

Was she courteous?

Did she make Mrs. Lane feel that the teacher and the class were glad to have visitors?

Did she make the introductions correctly?

II. Your teacher is a very busy person. She cannot always drop her work at a moment's notice and talk

with a visitor. Members of the class can be of real help in the classroom if each of them is prepared to greet a visitor courteously, make her feel entirely welcome, and carry on a pleasant conversation about the work the class is doing

If you do not have a hospitality committee in your class, choose girls and boys to form such a committee. You may wish to choose five persons so that the chairman may appoint one to serve each day in the week.

III. Choose three persons to take the part of the teacher, the visitor, and the member of the hospitality committee. Ask them to show how to receive a visitor. See whether they give the greeting and the introduction correctly, and whether they remember to extend other courtesies.

[ 117 ]

# MAKING INTRODUCTIONS

One morning Joe Lucas met a visitor in the hall of the school. She seemed to be looking for someone. Read the conversation that took place:

*Joe.* My name is Joe Lucas. May I help you?

*Visitor.* Thank you, Joe. I am Mrs. Daly, Frank's mother. Will you please show me the way to the principal's office?

*Joe.* I shall be glad to, Mrs. Daly. Have you met our principal?

*Mrs. Daly.* No, I haven't met him. This is my first visit here.

*Joe (entering the office door with Mrs. Daly).* Mrs. Daly, this is Mr. West, our principal. Mr. West, this is Mrs. Daly, Frank's mother.

Joe introduced Mr. West to Mrs. Daly. Usually introduce a man to a woman, or a boy to a girl; that is, say the woman's or the girl's name first.

Choose members of the class to introduce the following people:

1. A visitor, Mrs. Brown, and the principal, Mr. Harris
2. Your best friend, Sally Marr, and a classmate, Jerry Lake
3. Your teacher, Miss Smith, and a new pupil, Sam Todd
4. A new girl, Ann Sayre, and Miss Allen, the librarian

[ 118 ]

# CONVERSATION BY TELEPHONE

Read the following telephone conversation. Be ready to criticize the points you think incorrect.

*Mark (shouting).* Hello!

*Jane (in a faint voice).* Hello, who is this?

*Mark (still shouting).* I can't hear you!

*Jane (in a louder tone).* Mark, is it you?

*Mark (yelling).* Yes, it's Mark! Who are you?

*Jane.* I'm Jane Arnold. Don't yell like that.

*Mark (in a normal voice).* All right. Only I can't hear you half the time.

*Jane.* I guess 1 wasn't speaking directly into the mouthpiece. I was watching our cat. She is trying to catch a fly.

*Mark.* That's better. What do you want?

*Jane.* Is your sister Lucy there, Mark?

*Mark.* No.

*Jane.* When will she be back?

*Mark.* Oh, sometime soon, perhaps.

*Jane.* I was hoping she would be home. Well — uh — all right then. (*Pause.*) That's all I wanted to know. (*Pause.*) I think I had better hang up. Good-by.

[ 119 ]

By this time you are all ready to point out a great many mistakes in the conversation you have read. See how many you can point out.

Now read the following conversation between Larry and Ellen:

*Larry*. Hello. This is Larry Smith speaking.

*Ellen*. Hello, Larry. This is Ellen Lane. May I speak to Carol?

*Larry*. Carol isn't here right now, but she will be back in about an hour. Shall I have her call you when she comes in?

*Ellen*. Will you please do that, Larry? I would appreciate it very much. Good-by.

Point out the ways in which this second conversation is an improvement over the first one you read.

You may use the telephone often. It will pay you, now and then, to judge yourself by the standards given below.

---

### STANDARDS FOR TELEPHONING

1. Be courteous.
2. Have the right number when you place a call.
3. Tell at once who is speaking.
4. Be brief in giving your message or in answering a question, but tell enough to make further questions unnecessary.
5. Speak clearly and in a natural tone of voice.

---

Choose two persons to act out each of the following conversations:

1. Telephone the grocer to find out when a grocery order will be delivered.
2. Telephone Mary Brown's mother to find out why Mary has been absent from school.
3. Telephone a motion-picture theater to find out what time a certain picture begins.
4. Telephone a bus station to ask when the next bus leaves for a near-by town.

## THE TELEPHONE DIRECTORY

In a telephone directory, the names of persons and of businesses are arranged in alphabetical order. If you are looking for the name of a person, remember to look for the last name. When looking for the name of a company, look for the first important word in the company name. The word *the* before a company name is omitted in an alphabetical list.

1. List the following names in alphabetical order. Watch the first names and initials.

Martin, S. S.       Martin, C. L.       Martin, J. R.
Martin, Wm. C.      Martin, Alice       Martin, Nathan

2. List the following company names in the order of the alphabet:

The Caroline Candy Store      Taylor's Music Store
Vincent's Beauty Shop         The Rockville Theater
The Erie Railway Company      Lawrence Brothers

# SPEAKING CLEARLY

When you are with a friend, he can watch the movement of your lips as you talk. That helps him to understand what you say, even if you do not say each word distinctly. Since your friend cannot see you when you talk over a telephone, you must say every syllable clearly and distinctly.

I. Read aloud the following tongue twisters. Use your lips, teeth, and tongue to sound each word and syllable distinctly.

1. Six seasoned seamen sighted several seasick seals.
2. Thirteen thoughtless thieves threatened three thirsty thrushes.
3. Three two-toed tree toads trailed the throbbing train throttle.
4. Four frantic fishermen found five fresh fish.
5. When the whispering whistle whined, the white wheel whirred.

II. Practice reading this limerick until you can read it without a mistake:

A tutor who tooted a flute
Tried to teach two young tooters to toot;
   Said the two to the tutor,
    "Is it harder to toot, or
To tutor two tooters to toot?"

III. Make up a tongue twister. Read it aloud to the class.

## Practice with Sentences

1. Copy the sentences.  Put in the right word.

    1. The coach (says, said), "When the time-keeper (says, said) 'Go,' start running."

    2. "Jim (began, begun) to run before the time-keeper gave the signal," (says, said) Jack.

    3. "The boys (began, begun) the race quite slowly," Joe (said, says).

    4. "Now they have (begun, began) to run very fast," (said, says) Jack.

2. Write these sentences, putting in quotation marks, capital letters, and other punctuation marks:

    1. the speaker spoke too long,  Jim complained

    2. he didn't have a watch,  defended Joe

    3. Jerry spoke up,  shouldn't there be a clock in the auditorium

    4. some speakers need a calendar rather than a clock,  interrupted Jim.

3. Combine these pairs of short sentences.  Use such connecting words as *that, while, when, as, after.*

    1. This is the picture.  I drew.

    2. Jane got the cookies.  I got the milk.

    3. The plane pulled out.  Tuppy began to bark.

    4. I left the party.  I said good-by to Jane's mother.

    5. Dave skated to the store.  It began to rain.

# TAKING A TELEPHONE MESSAGE

Read the following telephone conversation:

*Mary.* Hello, this is Mary Gray.

*Mrs. Rich.* Hello, Mary. This is Mrs. Rich. Is your mother there?

*Mary.* I'm sorry, Mrs. Rich, but she is downtown, shopping. May I take a message?

*Mrs. Rich.* Do you think you can remember it, Mary? It is quite important.

*Mary.* I have paper and pencil here by the telephone. I'll write it down.

*Mrs. Rich.* That will help me a great deal, Mary. I have about fifteen other persons to call; so you can see why I wouldn't like to telephone a second time. Please tell your mother that the Hospital Board will meet December 4 at eight o'clock in the evening.

Who suggested that Mary take the message — Mrs. Rich or Mary? Did Mary have to leave the telephone to hunt for paper and pencil?

Look at the picture. Tell whether you think Mary made careful notes of the message.

# HOW WELL
# DO YOU REMEMBER?

If you make a mistake in a test, turn to page 126 or 127 and take the practice with the same number.

TEST I.   Use the right word in each sentence:

1. What has John (grew, grown) in his garden?
2. He (grew, growed) tomatoes and corn.
3. Hasn't he (growed, grown) any radishes?
4. George (growed, grew) a few radishes.

TEST II.   Copy each sentence.   Put in *flew* or *flown*.

1. Have the baby robins __?__ away yet?
2. Two of them __?__ from their nest today.
3. They __?__ back again.
4. The other three have not __?__ yet.

TEST III.   Use the right word in each sentence:

1. Bob (throwed, threw) the ball to first base.
2. Why hasn't Joe (threw, thrown) the ball?
3. There!   Joe has (thrown, threw) it now.
4. He (threw, throwed) it too late.

TEST IV.   Use the right word in each sentence:

1. Has the wind (blown, blew) hard recently?
2. It has (blew, blown) hard today.
3. Did you see the tree that the wind (blew, blowed) down yesterday?
4. The papers said it (blowed, blew) down a telephone pole today.

PRACTICE I.   *A.*  On page 104, review the verb forms *grew* and *grown.*

*B.*  Write each sentence, using the correct word:
1. Hasn't John (grew, grown) taller?
2. He has (growed, grown) taller than Joan.
3. During the past summer he (grew, growed) a half inch.
4. Mary (growed, grew) taller also.
5. These oranges were (grown, growed) in Florida.

PRACTICE II.  *A.* Read about *flew* and *flown* on page 104.

*B.*  Write each sentence, using *flew* or *flown:*
1. Have you __?__ your new kite yet?
2. I __?__ mine yesterday for the first time.
3. Joe has __?__ his kite every day this week.
4. The kite that Mark __?__ was new.
5. The young birds have __?__ from the nest.

PRACTICE III.  *A.* On page 104, read about *threw* and *thrown.*

*B.*  Copy each sentence.  Put in the right word.
1. Jack (threw, throwed) the ball into the basket.
2. How many times has he (threw, thrown) it?
3. Yesterday he (throwed, threw) it several times, but he always missed.
4. This is the first time he has (thrown, threw) it far enough.

[ 126 ]

PRACTICE IV. *A*. On page 104, review the verb forms *blew* and *blown*.

*B*. Write each sentence. Put in the correct word.

1. The policeman (blew, blowed) his whistle.
2. Hasn't he (blown, blew) it several times already?
3. He (blowed, blew) it at the motorist who parked his car near a fireplug.
4. That is the fifth time the policeman has (blew, blown) his whistle.

### Review Practice

Study this letter, noticing the capital letters and punctuation marks. Then write it as your teacher dictates it.

392 Glenbrook Drive
Northville, Indiana
March 12, 19—

Dear George,

Some of my friends and I have formed a club that meets every Friday. We call it the Junior Reading Club. Mrs. Murray, the librarian at the Northville Public Library, helps us.

Last month we read books about China. This month we are reading books about pioneer days in North America. The best story I have read recently is *Stocky, Boy of West Texas*, by Elizabeth W. Baker.

Your friend,
Jerry

[ 127 ]

# Unit Four

## ENJOYING BOOKS

## BOOKS OF LONG AGO

Here is a story that tells an experience of an Egyptian boy who lived in the days when books were very different from the books of today. Read it and try to imagine what he saw.

### BOOKMAKING IN ANCIENT EGYPT

Pepi (pā′pĭ) danced along at the side of his teacher, Seti (sā′tĭ). His short legs had to make two steps for every stride of Seti's.

"Why don't we run, Seti?" he inquired of his teacher. "Sethos (sā′thōs) might get tired of waiting for us and go away."

Seti laughed. "Sethos will be busy in his shop today and for many days to come. Yesterday, men brought to him many loads of papyrus (pa·pī′rŭs) plants from their farms in the Nile Delta of Egypt. Sethos is busy making the stalks of the plant into sheets that will be used to make scrolls (skrōls)."

"It is wonderful to hear you read from your scrolls about the building of our fine Egyptian temples," said Pepi quietly.

Just then Seti halted in front of a low shed made of sun-dried mud. "Here we are already," he said.

As the boy and his teacher walked about the large room, Pepi saw great piles of papyrus plants. The stalks were reeds as thick as a man's wrist and about fifteen feet in length. A number of men were working busily at them.

"This man is cutting the stalks into strips," the teacher pointed out. "That other one sorts the strips. Strips from the pith at the center of the stalks are the best."

"What is this man doing?" questioned Pepi.

"He is beating the strips with a copper hammer. That makes them soft so that they will bend easily," Seti replied.

[ 130 ]

One man was laying papyrus strips, which were about eighteen inches in length, in a row upon a sloping board over which water was trickling. When he had a row about twenty inches wide, he carefully placed other strips across them.

"But how will they stick together?" Pepi asked.

"The water draws out of the strips a sticky substance that will paste them together," said Seti.

The man pounded the strips to fasten them together more firmly into a sheet. Then he scraped the sheet to make it smooth, and later laid it in the sun to dry.

"See," said Seti. "There is another workman scraping and polishing the dried sheets with a piece of ivory."

Still another workman was picking up the finished sheets and trimming the rough edges. Then, by moistening the edges, he pasted a number of sheets together to form a long strip. Pepi watched him with great interest.

"Do you see the long strip?" asked Seti. "Look closely, and you will see how a scroll is made."

Each end of the long strip of papyrus was fastened to a brightly painted rod or roller. Then the strip was rolled around one of the rods.

"Now," said Seti, "there is a scroll, ready for a learned scribe (skrīb) to write upon."

Pepi was watching one of the most interesting processes ever invented. The Egyptians invented this process before the year 2500 B.C. Earlier than that, they had used an alphabet of twenty-four letters. But until the invention of writing material from papyrus, most early peoples carved their records on clay tablets or on stones.

Many hundreds of years later, in the Egyptian city of Alexandria, there was a great library containing many papyrus scrolls written by Egyptian scribes. The books in our own libraries of today do not look like the scrolls of early Egypt. But the paper contained in our books is made largely from plant fibers. It was the Egyptians who taught the world that plant fibers can produce a smooth, hard surface for writing, although the Chinese were the first to make paper as we know it today.

Later on, people learned to use parchment and vellum, made from the skins of animals.

I. Find the word *paper* in a large dictionary. See whether it comes from the Egyptian word *papyrus*.

II. The picture on page 128 shows what people of today think an early Egyptian library looked like.

How does it differ from our large city libraries of today?  In what ways is it like them?

In the picture, notice the scrolls stacked on shelves, the man reading from a scroll, and the scribe writing.

III. The pictures below show some early forms of books and records.  Study the pictures.

IV. The history of books and libraries is most interesting.  Would you like to know more about it?

Would you like to know how paper and books are made today?  Talk over these questions.

# PRONOUNCING VOWELS CORRECTLY

In the story you have just read, did you find some words that were new to you? To help you, each of these words was followed by aids in pronouncing. Here are the words and the pronouncing aids:

Pepi (pā′pǐ)                      papyrus (pa·pī′rŭs)
Seti (sā′tǐ)                      scroll (skrōl)
Sethos (sā′thōs)                 scribe (skrīb)

In the pronouncing aids, you see the mark (-) over certain vowels. This mark, called the *macron* (mā′-crŏn), tells you to "make the vowel say its own name." When you do, you are giving the *long sound* of the vowel.

Over some vowels in the pronunciation aids above, you see this mark (ˇ), called the *breve* (brēv). The breve gives a vowel the *short sound*.

Read aloud the two columns below. Listen for the difference between the long and short sound of each vowel.

| *Long Sounds* | *Short Sounds* |
|---|---|
| ā as in tāpe | ă as in tăp |
| ē as in mē | ĕ as in mĕt |
| ī as in hīde | ǐ as in hǐd |
| ō as in nōte | ŏ as in nŏt |
| ū as in hūge | ŭ as in hŭg |

Now look at the list of words at the top of the page. Say each word aloud, giving the vowels the correct sounds according to the marks shown in parentheses.

I. In the front part of most dictionaries there is a key to pronunciation. It is a list of all the letters in the alphabet, marked to show different sounds of the letters. Find this list in your dictionary. Look for the vowels in the list. How many different sounds has each vowel?

You now know about the macron (-) and the breve (ˇ). Look for the vowels that have these marks over them. Read aloud the line that tells how each vowel is sounded.

II. Find these words in your dictionary. In the pronunciation aid for each word, see the mark over the vowel and say the word aloud.

| scribe | run | bed | rob | scrape |
|--------|-----|-----|------|--------|
| scribble | rule | be | robe | scrap |

Did you notice that the *e's* at the end of *scribe, scribble, rule, robe,* and *scrape* were omitted in the pronunciation aids? That is because the *e* at the end of each of these words is a *silent letter*. It is not sounded.

III. Write this list on the blackboard. Place a mark over the vowel in each word to show how to sound it.

| map | we | us | fro | hill |
|-----|-----|-----|------|------|
| may | well | use | from | high |

IV. Find the following words in your dictionary. Study the pronunciation of each, read its meaning, and look at the picture, if there is one.

delta      temple      scroll      papyrus

## READING TO FIND OUT

If you decide to find out more about the beginnings of books and libraries, here are some suggestions that will help you. You will find other fact-finding aids on pages 137–141.

An author by the name of Rudyard Kipling wrote a book called *Just So Stories*. In the book are two stories (just make-believe tales) about how some early people began to write. The stories are entitled "How the Alphabet Was Made" and "How the First Letter Was Written." See whether you can find the book. Read the stories. They give some idea of how people happened to invent writing.

In many books of today you can read the story of the beginnings of writing and of books and libraries. Here is a list of some of them:

*Social Studies, Book One,* by Bruner and Smith
*Here Is a Book,* by Marshall McClintock
*Story of Books up through the Ages,* by Marjorie Maxwell
*Books and Their History,* by R. N. D. Wilson
*Words on Wings,* by Lillian J. Bragdon

# USING AN ENCYCLOPEDIA

Do you ever think of an encyclopedia as a set of books with which you can have a good time? Encyclopedias for boys and girls are interesting to read, and have many pictures that you will enjoy.

As you hunt for facts about the history of books and libraries, be sure to look for encyclopedias in your classroom library, your school library, and the public library. Here are the titles of some of them:

*Britannica Junior*
*Compton's Pictured Encyclopedia*
*The World Book Encyclopedia*

If you find one of these encyclopedias, use the following suggestions to aid you in your search:

1. Look at the backs of all the volumes (books) in the set and notice the letter or letters. They tell you the first letter of all topics in that volume.

2. Have ready a list of topics that you wish to look for, such as this:

| | | |
|---|---|---|
| Books | Alphabet | Paper |
| Bookmaking | Papyrus | Writing |
| Libraries | | Egypt |

A good list of topics supplies you with a number of clues. You have to be a good detective to think of all the clues and follow them.

3. When you find a topic such as *Libraries*, in an encyclopedia, notice how many pages are given to it.

You may not care to read all these pages; so you must think of more clues to guide you in your search.

For example, in an article on the topic *Libraries*, you may find a subtopic such as *History of Libraries*. That part you will wish to read.

If you do not find subtopics, skim over the article. Look at the first sentence or two in each paragraph to learn the topic of the paragraph. Read only the paragraphs that give you what you are looking for.

4. Sometimes the encyclopedia gives you other good clues. In an article on *Books*, you may find a suggestion, such as "See *Babylon*," or "See *Writing*," or "See *Alphabet*," or "See *Paper*." The encyclopedia is telling you that you may find more facts by turning to other topics.

5. The pictures will give you much help. Study them closely. Read the legends beneath the pictures.

If you follow these suggestions, you will find encyclopedias interesting and entertaining book friends. Learn to be a good fact detective. Use all the clues that will be useful to you.

# USING GUIDE WORDS

To be successful in using the encyclopedia, you must know alphabetical order. These exercises will test your skill.

I. Like the dictionary, the encyclopedia has *guide words* at the top of all pages. They will help you to find your topic.

Suppose you open the *A* volume to a page having the guide word *Ant* at the top. Tell whether you will turn toward the front or the back of the book to find each of these topics:

| | | |
|---|---|---|
| Alphabet | Australia | Arizona |
| Amber | Addition | Aquarium |
| Asia | Aircraft | Apple |

II. Write the list of words above in alphabetical order. To do this, you will have to look at the second letter of each word.

III. When you look for the topic *Library*, you find a great many pages that have guide words beginning with *Li*. Perhaps the first one you look at has the guide word *Lighthouse* on it. Does *Library* come before or after *Lighthouse*?

Which of these topics come before *Lighthouse*:

| | | |
|---|---|---|
| Liberia | Literature | Lieutenant |
| Licorice | Lion | Lisbon |
| Lizard | Light | Lincoln |

IV. Write the words listed above in alphabetical order. Watch the third letter of each word.

# LEARNING TO SKIM

Here is an article about the papyrus plant. Before reading it closely, follow the directions given here:

1. Take a sheet of paper. At the top write the title of the article. Then write Roman numbers from I to IV in a column.

2. Now, skim over the opening sentence or two of the first paragraph, decide the main topic, and write it after number I on your paper.

Next, skim over the opening sentences of the second paragraph, decide what the topic of the paragraph is, and write it beside number II.

Do the same with the other two paragraphs.

## EGYPTIAN PAPYRUS

Papyrus is a reedlike water plant that grows in the delta of the Nile River in Egypt. Its tall, straight stems grow to a height of ten to twenty feet. The leaves of the plant cluster about the base of the stems, and the flowers grow from their tips.

The early Egyptians used the papyrus plant for many purposes. From the stems they made boats. From the fiber they wove maps and sailcloth. The pith, or core of the stem, was cooked and eaten as food. The wood of the root was used as fuel and to make household utensils. But the most important use of papyrus was the making of writing material that was a forerunner of our paper.

Writing material made from the papyrus plant had many uses. Some of it was made into scrolls or books. But much of it was used for everyday purposes, such as writing letters or invitations, making out tax bills and receipts, and keeping the accounts of shopkeepers. Laws were copied on sheets of papyrus, and public officials also kept their records on this writing material.

For many years Egypt guarded the secret of making writing material from papyrus. She even refused to supply other countries with papyrus. For this reason, substitutes for it had to be found. In time people began to use the skin of sheep to make parchment, and the skin of calves to make vellum, both of which were used to make books.

3. Look at the list of topics that you prepared in exercises 1 and 2. Tell which paragraph (or paragraphs) you would read closely to find the answer to each of the following questions:

    1. Did other countries in early days use papyrus paper?
    2. What was the papyrus plant like?
    3. For what purposes was papyrus used as paper?
    4. Was the plant used for purposes other than papermaking?

4. Now read all the paragraphs closely and write the answers to the questions asked in the exercise above.

# HOW THE LIBRARY HELPS YOU

If you plan to go to your school library for one or more of the books listed on page 136, are you sure you know how to find them?

Sometimes you may ask the librarian for a book you wish to read. But if you know how to use library aids, you do not need to depend on the librarian.

## Using the card catalogue

In every library there is a card catalogue. It is a case of small drawers, such as you see in the picture below. The case contains one or more cards for each book in the library. The cards are arranged in alphabetical order, and on the front of each drawer are one or more letters.

## Finding an author card

Suppose you are looking for *Story of Books up through the Ages*, by Marjorie Maxwell. You must find a card headed *Maxwell, Marjorie;* so you look

for a drawer marked *M*, or perhaps *Ma*, or perhaps *Ma-Mo*. Tip forward the cards so marked until you come to *Max*, then to *Maxwell, Marjorie*. You may see on the card something like this:

```
X 655   Maxwell, Marjorie
M 45

        Story of Books up through the Ages
```

The numbers in the upper left corner tell you where to find the book. Ask the librarian or your teacher to explain how the numbers quickly guide you to the book.

## Finding a subject card

You may not happen to know of any books that tell about the making of paper today. Then you can look in the drawer marked *P* (or *Pa*) and find a card with the subject *Paper* at the top. Following it, you will find cards that tell you the title and author of each book in the library that tells about papermaking. In one corner of each card is a number that tells you how to find the book.

## Using other library aids

If you cannot find *reference books*, such as encyclopedias, the librarian will show you where they are.

If you wish pictures of early books and libraries, ask the librarian to find some in the *picture file*.

Be sure to make your request courteously and to thank the librarian for any help she gives you.

[ 143 ]

During a class conversation one day, Jack mentioned a good book he was reading.

"What's the title of the book?" asked Ted.

"Oh, I don't remember," answered Jack. "It's about Indians. You ought to read it."

"Why do you like it?" Nancy wanted to know.

"I don't know," Jack replied.

"You can't like a book and not have a reason for it," explained Nancy. "And you ought to be able to tell a little about the book, so that we can decide whether we want to read it."

"If you will give me a little time, perhaps I can tell you about it," Jack answered.

The class agreed to do this.

"Suppose all of you plan reports about interesting books you have read recently," Miss Green suggested to the class. "Then we can have a number of short book reports."

"We could pretend that we are trying to sell our books," suggested Bob.

Edna St. Vincent Millay

Robert P. Tristram
Coffin

Mary Ellen  Chase

"That's a good idea, Bob," said Miss Green. "I'll give you book salesmen ten minutes to think about your books. When the time is up, be ready to give your sales talk to the class!"

Since the boys and girls were curious about Jack's book, he gave his report first. Here it is:

The best book I have read recently is an Indian story called *Younger Brother, A Cherokee Indian Tale*, written by Charlie May Simon.

Among the Cherokee Indians, the men of the tribe call the growing boys "younger brothers." The chief characters in the book, Sungi and Bullhead, were boys of the same age. But Bullhead grew tall and strong, while Sungi remained thin and undersized. This gave Bullhead an excuse for calling Sungi "younger brother."

But Sungi's courage was strong. When the chance came, he led an attack on the Creek Indians and recovered some stolen goods. When he also had captured a prisoner of war, Sungi proved that he was no longer a "younger brother."

I liked the book partly because Indian stories are my favorites, and partly because Bullhead and Sungi had such interesting experiences. If you enjoy a fine Indian story, be sure to read this book.

[ 145 ]

The class thought Jack's report very good, and they told him so. Several of the boys decided at once to read *Younger Brother*.

See whether you can tell why Jack's report was good by answering these questions:

1. Did he give you a good idea of what the book was about?
2. Did he name the title and author?
3. Did he tell too much of the story, or too little?
4. Did he make the book seem so interesting that you wish to read it yourself?

Probably each of you reads many good books. Just as you enjoy telling your friends about other good times, you will enjoy telling them of your good times with a book. Plan a time each week when some of you may give reports on good books.

Here are some suggestions that will help you make a good report.

---

**STANDARDS FOR GIVING A BOOK REPORT**

1. Be sure to give the exact title of the book and the name of the author.
2. Tell what the book is about.
3. Tell only enough of the story to make your listeners wish to know more.
4. Make them feel that you truly enjoyed reading the book.

---

After Miss Green's class had given their reports, they decided that Nancy had the best sales talk. Read her report. Then tell whether you think it meets the standards on page 146.

Poor Esmeralda! How unhappy she was! To begin with, she was a princess, with a beautiful palace for a home and many servants to wait on her. She had lovely clothes to wear and wonderful things to eat. Still she spent a great deal of her time crying. Can you guess why? She cried because people called her Esmeralda the Plain.

Finally her father, the king, decided that something must be done about it. He put this advertisement in the paper:

Anyone capable of transforming a plain young lady into a beautiful young lady will be given a purse of gold. Results must be guaranteed. Those failing will lose their heads.

People did not want to lose their heads, so nobody applied — that is, nobody except one poor woman. She claimed that she could make the princess beautiful, but asked that the princess come to live with her for six months.

If you would like to know how Esmeralda the Plain became Esmeralda the Beautiful, you must get the book from the school library and read it. Its title is *The Plain Princess*. Phyllis McGinley is the author.

"Oh, Nancy, don't quit now!" cried Beth when Nancy had finished.

"Please tell us how the princess became beautiful," begged Rose. "I don't see how I can wait until I get to the library."

"Don't you let anybody tease you into telling the ending, Nancy," said Miss Green. Then she turned to the class and said, "You see, boys and girls, that Nancy did just what she set out to do. She gave her report so well that some of the rest of you want to read the book."

Do you agree that Nancy's report was a better sales talk than Jack's? If you do, be able to give some reasons why you think so.

## CHECKING A SPEAKER

At the close of your book-report period, think how well each speaker delivered his report. Say *Yes* or *No* to each of the questions below:

1. Did he stand tall and straight?
2. Did he look directly at his audience?
3. Did he speak clearly and loudly?
4. Did he keep his sentences apart, and not string them together with *and-a* or *er-er?*
5. Did he use correct words?

[ 148 ]

# USING A AND AN

Are you always careful to use *an* when you should? Notice these expressions from Jack's report:

*an* Indian story      *a* prisoner of war
*an* attack          *a* fine Indian story

*An* should be used before words beginning with the vowels *a, e, i, o,* and the short sound of *ŭ:*

*an* airport        *an* old friend
*an* engine        *an* uncle
*an* idle fellow     *an* ugly duckling

*An* should also be used before words beginning with silent *h,* such as:

*an* heir     *an* honest boy     *an* hour

Use *a* before all words beginning with consonants that are sounded, and before words beginning with the long sound of *ū,* such as:

*a* home     *a* king     *a* uniform     *a* useful gift

Read the following sentences, using *a* or *an* in place of the blanks:

1. I have just read __?__ interesting story about __?__ explorer.
2. The hero of my book has __?__ airplane accident and __?__ thrilling rescue.
3. Joe borrowed __?__ uniform from __?__ uncle of his.
4. The boys made __?__ house for the lost baby squirrel in less than __?__ hour.

# BUILDING A BOOK LIST

Do you often wonder what book to read next? It is a good plan to list the titles and authors of books you hear or read about.

Here are some suggestions which will help you build a list of interesting reading materials:

1. During your class book-review period, keep your Language Notebook before you. On a page headed Books I Wish to Read, write the title of each good book you hear about. Write the name of the author as well as the place where you may get the book.

2. Magazines for children often give a page or two of book reviews. If you take such a magazine, read the book reviews. Add to the list in your Language Notebook the title and author of any good book that the reviews suggest.

If you do not take a magazine, find children's magazines in the magazine rack at the library. Look for book reviews in them.

3. Ask the librarian of your school or of the public library whether she has a list of books for boys and girls of your age. If there is such a list, choose from it the titles and authors of books you think you would like to read and add them to your own list.

Keep your list of books growing. Try to list books of different kinds. As you learn to enjoy many kinds of books, you will get more pleasure from your reading, both in and out of school.

# WRITING A BOOK LIST

As you add to your book list, be sure to write the book titles and the authors' names correctly. Notice the capital letters in the following:

*Story of a Bad Boy,* by J. B. Aldrich

What rules for capital letters does this title follow?

Write the following titles correctly:

the goldsmith of florence, by katharine gibson

liners and freighters, by wilson starbuck

the chinese ink stick, by kurt wiese

## Reviewing Correct Words

Write each sentence and put in the correct word:

1. The candle (throwed, threw) a ray of light into the cave.
2. The bats had (flew, flown) from the cave before we reached it.
3. A big gust of wind (blowed, blew) out the sputtering candle.
4. Mushrooms are often (grown, growed) in caves.
5. The explosion had (blew, blown) a huge rock from the cliff.
6. The air (grew, growed) colder as the boys went deeper into the cave.
7. Joe had (throwed, thrown) a stone into the lake to hear the echo.

# WRITING A BOOK REVIEW

Bob read this review in a copy of *Junior Natural History Magazine:*

McCulloch, Robert W., *Come, Jack!*

This is a dog story that fills the reader with almost breathless excitement from start to finish. The dog hero has adventures that begin on a farm in West Virginia and take him to the prairie lands of Nebraska. He frees himself from a villain who robs and nearly kills his master, and, in the strange new land of the West, learns to fight wild animals — from coyotes to rattlesnakes.

Does this review make you eager to read the book it describes?

I. In the review on the opposite page, West Virginia is written in full. It is never correct to use an abbreviation in a sentence.

II. Perhaps your class would like to keep a file of short book reviews written by members of the class. Such a file will help the class in two important ways:

Writing the card will help each of you to express a definite opinion of a book you have read.

The file will aid you in choosing good books to read. If anyone wishes to know of a good book quickly, he can go through the file until he finds a review that interests him.

Here are suggestions for making a file:

1. Get a package of $5\frac{1}{2}''$ by $8''$ cards.

2. Get a box to hold the cards.

3. Make guide cards for the twenty-six letters of the alphabet.

4. Whenever you finish a book, write a very brief paragraph about it. The one on page 152 is a good model for you to follow.

When you are sure your sentences, capitalization, and punctuation are correct, copy the review on a card. At the top of the card write the author's name, with the last name first. Under it write the title of the book. Be sure to sign your name to your review.

5. Give your cards to your librarian, who should file them in alphabetical order by the authors' last names.

## Practice in Checking

Here is Henry's report on *Paddlewings* by Wilfrid Bronson. Find all the mistakes Henry made. Then write the report correctly.

Although this is a story about a penguin. It tells a great deal more than you wood think. Since penguins live on islands, the author tells how animals and birds came to live on islands. He also tells a grate deal about other animal life.

## SPELLING WORDS CORRECTLY

In Henry's report did you notice that he wrote *wood* for *would* and *grate* for *great?*

Always be on the lookout for words that sound alike but are spelled differently and have different meanings.

Explain the difference in the meanings of the words in each pair below. If necessary, use your dictionary.

| wood | grate | hole | pair | bear |
|------|-------|------|------|------|
| would | great | whole | pare | bare |
| pour | pale | made | bow | toe |
| pore | pail | maid | bough | tow |

Choose five of these pairs of words that you find difficult. Write a sentence containing each of the ten words. Be sure to choose the right spelling for the meaning you have in mind.

# SINGULAR AND PLURAL NOUNS

The name of a person, an animal, an object, or a place is called a *noun*.

A noun may name one or more than one. A noun that names one person or object is called a *singular* noun. *Singular* comes from the word *single*, which means one. A noun that names more than one is called a *plural* noun.

Read these singular and plural nouns. Notice how the spelling of each singular noun changes in order to make the plural form.

| *Singular Nouns* | *Plural Nouns* |
|---|---|
| penguin | penguins |
| island | islands |
| fox | foxes |
| dish | dishes |
| pony | ponies |
| man | men |
| child | children |
| knife | knives |

Some nouns are the same in the singular and plural forms. You say, "one deer" or "a herd of ten deer." You also say, "one sheep" or "a dozen sheep."

When you are not sure of the spelling of the plural form of a noun, turn to your dictionary. It will give you the plural of any noun that does not form its plural by adding *s* or *es*. For example, after the word *city*, you will find "*pl.* CITIES"; after the word *half*, you will find "*pl.* HALVES."

1. Find each of the following nouns in the dictionary. Learn how to spell its plural form. Then use the plural in a sentence.

| | | | |
|---|---|---|---|
| city | loaf | dwarf | navy |
| valley | ox | woman | buffalo |

2. It is right to use *is* and *isn't, was* and *wasn't,* with singular nouns. It is right to use *are* and *aren't,* *were* and *weren't,* with plural nouns.

Read each sentence below. Think whether the noun that names what the sentence is talking about is singular or plural. Then read the sentence with the right word in it.

1. (Isn't, Aren't) this *book* a new one?
2. Our new *books* (are, is) on the top shelf.
3. (Wasn't, Weren't) John's *report* interesting?
4. (Aren't, Isn't) the *pictures* in this book fine?
5. (Aren't, Isn't) this *magazine* in the library?
6. *Joe and Anne* (wasn't, weren't) ready to give their reports.
7. (Weren't, Wasn't) the *boys* interested in that book?

3. Write the plural of each of these nouns:

| | | | |
|---|---|---|---|
| goose | baby | bush | elf |
| key | box | sheep | lady |

Use your dictionary to check the spelling of the plurals you have written.

[ 156 ]

# WRITING SINGULAR POSSESSIVES

Read the following sentence:

The penguin's home is on an island.

The noun *penguin's* shows ownership, or possession. It is the *possessive form* of the singular noun *penguin*.

To make a singular noun show possession, add an apostrophe and *s* (*'s*).

1. Name the possessive nouns in the following sentences. Notice that each is a singular noun. Tell how each possessive form is made.

1. Miss Johnson's class invited us to their radio program.
2. The captain of the team praised each boy's work.
3. Tom and Anne are on James's committee.
4. Alice's picture was voted the best.
5. On Saturdays I work in my father's store.
6. I have read that author's book.

2. Write each sentence and put in the possessive form of each singular noun in parentheses:

1. Are you going to (Joe) house after school?
2. I like (Andersen) fairy tales the best.
3. (Grace) poem is very clever.
4. Have you read (Louisa M. Alcott) books?
5. I like to read the stories about (King Arthur) brave knights.
6. You must take the book to the (librarian) desk as soon as possible.

# WRITING PLURAL POSSESSIVES

A plural noun also may show possession.   Read these sentences and notice the possessive plural nouns:

1. The *girls'* costumes are ready.
2. We went to the little *children's* assembly.

Read the following rules:

When the plural form of a noun ends in *s*, the possessive is formed by adding the apostrophe only.

When the plural form of a noun does not end in *s*, add both the apostrophe and *s* to form the possessive.

Study these forms of plural nouns:

| Plural | Possessive | Plural | Possessive |
|--------|-----------|--------|-----------|
| boys | boys' coats | men | men's hats |

1. Form the possessives of these plural nouns:

| | | | |
|--------|--------|--------|--------|
| mothers | geese | hens | babies |
| women | girls | men | ponies |

2. Write each sentence and put in the possessive form of the plural noun in parentheses:

1. On the (twins) birthday we went to the County Fair.
2. We walked slowly past the (horses) stalls.
3. The (women) sewing exhibit was very fine.
4. The (clowns) performances were very funny.
5. Bob and I entered the (boys) races.
6. The (dairymen) exhibit was interesting.

## APPLYING FOR A LIBRARY CARD

If you wish to borrow books from the public library, the librarian will give you an *application blank.*

Here is a blank that Susan Hall filled and returned to the library.   Read it carefully.

---

    I hereby apply for the privileges of the Yonkers Public Library.   I promise to obey its rules and to pay all fines or damages charged to me.   I will report to the librarian if I move.

Name.. *Susan Hall* ............

Home Address.. *15 Greenvale Avenue*

School.. *16* .......... Grade *5 B* Age *10*

Signature of Parent. *G. K. Hall* .......

Signature of Teacher. *Marion Green* ....

       Yonkers, New York. *Jan. 7,* 19*48*.

---

# A RADIO GAME

Have you ever listened to a *What's-My-Name?* program on the radio? On such a program, the speaker gives a description and the audience guesses who or what has been described.

Plan a "radio program" of this kind. Each member of the class may write a short description of a well-known book character and read it aloud. The rest of the class may guess who is described.

Here is a description that Bob gave:

> I live in a small village on the banks of the Mississippi River. Although I don't think I am an unusually bad boy, I am always getting into trouble. Once a friend and I were lost in a cave, but we found our way out again. Then another friend and I found a treasure in the cave. *What's My Name?*

Can you guess the name of the character Bob described? Is it Tom Sawyer?

Here is the description Rose gave. See whether you can guess the name.

My home is in New England. I live there with my three sisters and Marmee, our mother. Next door to us live an old friend and his grandson. Although we do not have much money, my sisters and I have many good times together and are very happy. *What's My Name?*

If you plan to have a *What's My Name?* program, follow these suggestions:

1. Choose a leading character from a book that many of your class have read. Think of three or four facts about that character. Then write a good paragraph about the character, using these facts.

2. Practice reading your paragraph so that you can read it without stumbling over the words.

3. When you step to the microphone, read your description clearly and in a pleasing voice.

# MORE BOOK REVIEWS

Does your town newspaper have a column of children's book reviews? Some papers do. These reviews are often written by boys and girls who send them directly to the book-review editor. Would you like to see your reviews in print?

Write a class letter to the editor, asking him if he will start such a column. Turn to page 226 for help in writing your letter.

## Check Test 6: Correct Words

1. Write each sentence. Put in the correct word:

    1. Jay's father (let, left) him sleep in the tent.
    2. Will you (leave, let) me read your book about rocket planes?
    3. The boys (drew up, drawed up) plans for a new club.
    4. Has Anne (drawn, drawed) a partner?
    5. Dick has (drawn, drew) a comic strip for our newspaper.
    6. I can't find (those, them) cards.

2. Write each sentence and leave out the unnecessary word:

    1. The rocket planes they haven't any pilot.
    2. The hero of the book he is an Indian guide.
    3. This model it flies faster than any others.
    4. Tom and I we take a hike each Saturday.

Turn to page 283 for further help.

# HOW WELL
# DO YOU REMEMBER?

Take these tests to find out how well you remember what you learned in Unit Four. If you make a mistake in any test, turn to pages 165–166 and take the practice with the same number.

TEST I. *A.* Write these encyclopedia topics in alphabetical order. Watch the third letter in each word.

| Man | Maple | Maine |
| Magic | Madison | Major |
| March | Mason | Matches |

*B.* Put these topics in alphabetical order. Watch the fourth letter in each.

| Shale | Shaft | Shamrock |
| Shakespeare | Shadows | Shanghai |
| Shawl | Shasta | Shark |

TEST II. Write the following sentences, using *a* or *an* wherever you find a blank:

1. *The Mystery of the Old Barn*, by Mary Urmston, tells about __?__ adventure in __?__ old barn.
2. Judy, Mark, and Roger spent __?__ entire summer on __?__ farm.
3. They heard __?__ creak in __?__ empty loft.
4. While they were watching, __?__ airplane from Mark's model collection disappeared from sight.
5. Someone threw __?__ rock from __?__ ambush.

[ 163 ]

TEST III. Write the plural forms of these nouns:

foot      army      calf      fly
dress      library      potato      alley

TEST IV. In each sentence is a singular noun in parentheses. Write the sentence and make that noun show possession.

1. (Bob) language book fell to the floor.
2. The best thing on our assembly program was (Jane) story.
3. The little (girl) doll was broken.
4. Joe found the (policeman) whistle.
5. We all liked (James) report.
6. The (woman) dress was pretty.

TEST V. *A.* Write the possessive forms of these plural nouns:

geese      mice      peaches      monkeys
ladies      deer      giants      oxen

*B.* In each sentence there is a plural noun in parentheses. Write the sentence and make that noun show possession.

1. We enjoyed the (firemen) parade.
2. The store sells (boys) hats.
3. There are seven players on the (girls) team.
4. In the (lions) cage were a lion, a lioness, and a cub.
5. Where can we find the (children) books?
6. Mother went to the (babies) department in the local store.

[ 164 ]

PRACTICE I.  *A.*  Review page 139.

*B.*  Write the following topics in alphabetical order. Watch the third letter in each word.

    Church       Chivalry      Chopin

    Charles      Christmas    Cheetah

              Chlorine

*C.*  Write these topics in alphabetical order.  Look at the fourth letter in each.

Trapping     Tractor      Trade      Traffic

Trailer       Tramway     Travel     Transport

PRACTICE II.  *A.*  Read about *a* and *an* on page 149.

*B.*  Write these sentences, putting in *a* and *an:*

1. *Children of the Housetops* is __?__ story of Persia.
2. I read a good story of __?__ Indian pony.
3. Have you read *Polaris,* a story of __?__ Eskimo dog?
4. *Katrinka* is the story of __?__ Russian child.
5. My favorite book is about __?__ airplane pilot.
6. Have you read *Talking Bird?*  It is __?__ Aztec story.

PRACTICE III.  *A.*  On pages 155–156 read about the singular and plural forms of nouns.

*B.*  Copy these sentences, changing the singular nouns in parentheses to plural nouns:

1. Put the (tomato) on the table.
2. Dave caught four (trout).

3. Set the (box) on the floor.
4. Take the (class) to the library.
5. Place the (chair) against the wall.
6. Read the (story) to the class.

PRACTICE IV.   A. On page 157 review how to write the possessive form of a singular noun.

B. Write each sentence, using the possessive form of the noun in parentheses:

1. (Charles) sweater is new.
2. Have you found (Miss Smith) book?
3. What is the (author) name?
4. I enjoy reading (Mark Twain) book.
5. The (hero) home was in Indiana.

PRACTICE V.   A. On page 158 review how to write the possessive forms of plural nouns.

B. Write the possessive form of each of these plural nouns:

babies      women      children
wolves      men        robins

C. Write each sentence, using the possessive form of the plural noun in parentheses:

1. Put the (pupils) books on the shelf.
2. The boy found the (spies) secret papers.
3. Take the (children) parents to the auditorium.
4. The (ponies) manes are very shaggy.
5. Everyone praised the (players) excellent team-work.

1. Read each sentence and decide which word in parentheses is the correct one to use. Then write the sentence.

    1. Yesterday John (says, said) he was not going on the hike.
    2. The boys (begun, began) to cross the bridge.
    3. When Ruth came in, no one (says, said) a word to her.
    4. The band has (began, begun) to play.
    5. Have you (begun, began) to keep a reading record?

2. Decide which of the following are sentences. Make a sentence out of each group that does not express a complete thought. Write the sentences.

    1. As soon as Agnes is ready.
    2. Put the plant on the window sill.
    3. Sitting on a twig and singing cheerily.
    4. The brave knight riding a black horse.
    5. He rode into the deep forest.

3. Check this paragraph and find the mistakes. Then write it correctly.

jemima was a little pioneer made she could keep house and so. She could cook a bare steak as well as her mother could her father, Daniel Boone, taught her how to shoot. Once jemima was captured by the indians.

# Unit Five

## MAKING REPORTS

### CELEBRATING HOLIDAYS

The word *holiday* was formed by combining the two words *holy* and *day*. In ancient times most holidays were church days. Some were in honor of religious events. Christmas and Easter are holidays of this kind. Other holidays honored important religious leaders or saints. A number of religious holidays are still celebrated.

There are also holidays on which we celebrate historical events and the birthdays of famous national heroes. Independence Day, or Fourth of July, and Washington's Birthday are days of historical importance.

In some sections of our country and in some states, there are holidays to celebrate events that are of interest only to the people of that section or state. Lee's Birthday, celebrated in the South, and Forefathers' Day, celebrated in New England, are holidays of this kind.

Besides the holidays, there are special days such as Saint Patrick's Day, Halloween, and Saint Valentine's Day. The celebrations on these days do honor to old beliefs and customs. In school you often celebrate the birthdays of great authors or scientists, and other special days such as Arbor Day, Bird Day, and Flag Day.

Do you know the history or legends behind most of our holidays and special days? Why do we have a tree at Christmas time? Who were Saint Valentine and Saint Patrick? Why does New England celebrate Forefathers' Day? How did Bird Day, Arbor Day, and Flag Day begin, and why do we celebrate them now?

If you would like to know the answers to such questions, plan a study of our holidays and of other special days and anniversaries.

I. First, make a class list of all the important days you celebrate. Include in your list the true holidays and also the special days.

II. Next, choose a committee to search in your own library and in the public library, to find books that tell about holidays and festivals, and list these books. They should use the card catalogue in the public library to help them in their search.

The committee should place on a table or on a separate shelf in your classroom library the books they can find.

Each of you might examine your reader and your history text to see what help they can give you.

The following books tell about the celebration of holidays and special days in our country. Your committee might look for them in your school or your public library.

Curtis, Mary I., *Why We Celebrate Our Holidays*

Graham, Eleanor, *Happy Holidays*

McSpadden, Joseph W., *Book of Holidays*

Sechrist, Elizabeth H., *Red Letter Days*

Notice that the name of each author is given first, with the title of the book following it. Are the last names of the authors in alphabetical order?

In writing the book list, the committee should follow this form. What rules for capital letters and punctuation marks do they need to remember?

III. Each girl and boy should choose one holiday from the list the class has prepared. Then everyone should follow these steps:

1. Look over the books that the committee has gathered, examining the tables of contents and indexes to see which ones have facts about the holiday chosen.
2. Read the pages that tell about that holiday.
3. Take notes on the most interesting facts.
4. Make an outline from the notes.
5. Plan a report to be given to the class.

In the next few days take the lessons on pages 172–178. They will help you to prepare a good report.

# TAKING NOTES

Don chose May Day for his topic. He looked at the tables of contents and indexes of the books that the committee had collected, and he found a book that told about May Day.

Because he wished to remember the main facts that he read, Don made some notes in his notebook. They are shown on the opposite page. Read them before you answer the questions below:

I. What did Don write at the top of his page? Why is it a good plan to list the title and author of the book and the pages read?

II. Did Don write whole sentences or just groups of words as reminders?

III. Did Don group together the facts about each topic? What are his main topics?

As you read about a holiday, take notes on the main facts. It will help you to remember them and to plan a good report.

Follow these suggestions:

1. Write first the title of the book (or encyclopedia) and list the page numbers.
2. Jot down words or groups of words to use as reminders.
3. Group the facts under main topics if you can.

McSpadden, Joseph W., *Book of Holidays*
May Day, pages 105-115

Old Roman festival in honor of Flora,
   goddess of spring and flowers
   Children danced in streets—wreaths on heads
   Twined garlands around columns of temple
   Put flowers on altar

May Day also celebrated in England
   People up after midnight—went to woods
     for branches and flowers
   Parade of stagecoaches trimmed with
     flowers
   Parade and feast of chimney sweeps
   Children hung wreaths on doorknobs
   Great event—Maypole dance

In our country not widely celebrated
   Some schools have May festivals with
     folk dances and Maypole
   May baskets made by some children

# MAKING AN OUTLINE

Before Don gave his report to the class, he made an outline of the facts he had jotted down in his notebook. Here is his outline:

### The Story of May Day

I. Roman festival in honor of Flora

    A. Parade of dancing children

    B. Decoration of temple and altar

II. English festival

    A. Early rising to gather flowers

    B. Parade of decorated stagecoaches

    C. Parade and feast of chimney sweeps

    D. Maypole dances

III. Celebration in United States

    A. School festivals

    B. May baskets

I. Compare this outline with Don's notes on page 173. How did his notes help him to make a good outline for his report?

II. Why do you think this outline helped Don to make a good report? Where did he use capital letters and punctuation marks?

III. Before you give your report, study your notes carefully. Make an outline of the points you wish to tell. Then practice giving your report, using your outline as a guide.

# ADDING TO YOUR VOCABULARY

As you read about the holiday you chose, give special attention to the new words you find. Try to use them in your report. They will make your report more interesting.

I. Here are some words and expressions you might wish to use if you talk about May Day:

| | |
|---|---|
| ancient custom | erected a Maypole |
| gay finery | out-of-door festivities |
| twined the pillars | flower-decked procession |

Do you know what these words and expressions mean? If not, use your dictionary to find out. Then use each expression in a sentence that tells about a May Day custom.

II. Here are some more words you will often use as you talk about holidays. Find each word in the dictionary. Study the syllables and accent marks. Then learn to pronounce the word correctly.

| | | |
|---|---|---|
| anniversary | festival | religious |
| celebration | legal | patriotic |
| observance | original | recognized |

Use each of these words in a sentence that tells about one of our holidays.

III. When you find good new words and have mastered them, put them in your Language Notebook. Then plan to use them in your report.

Using both his notes and his outline, Don prepared his May Day report.   Here is the report he gave to the class:

The celebration of May Day is an ancient custom.   In early days the Romans had a festival in honor of Flora, goddess of spring and flowers.   It lasted from April 28 to May 1.   Children wove wreaths of flowers and put them on their heads.   They went dancing about the streets.   Older boys and girls twined garlands around the pillars of the Temple of Flora and decorated the altar with flowers.   According to a legend of the time, the first one to place flowers on the altar would be the first to marry.

After the Romans conquered England, the celebration of May Day became an English custom.   Just after midnight many people got up and went to the forests to gather branches and flowers.   Some of them decorated the stagecoaches with flowers and had a parade.   The chimney sweeps dressed up and paraded, too, and the rich people gave them a feast.   Many children filled small baskets with flowers and hung them on the doorknobs of their friends' homes.

The biggest event was the Maypole dance. Some men erected a Maypole in the center

of the village green. The women twined garlands of flowers about it and strung gay ribbons from the top. Then the young men and maidens danced around the Maypole.

English settlers brought their May Day customs to our country. Today many children in our country celebrate May Day. In some towns schools have Maypole dances and other folk dances in the parks. In many schools the children make May baskets and fill them with flowers. Whether we celebrate it or not, we all like May Day because it brings back the trees and flowers.

Do you like Don's report? Compare it with the outline on page 174. Did Don tell his facts in order?

When you plan your report, follow the outline you made. That will help you to keep your facts in order. Use the following standards to guide you in your planning.

---

STANDARDS FOR AN ORAL REPORT
1. Tell the facts in order.
2. Use interesting words and expressions that you learned through your reading.
3. Speak clearly.
4. Let your voice show that you are interested in what you are telling.

---

# SPECIAL FESTIVALS

Many towns or sections of our country have special celebrations of their own.   Some of them are festivals held in honor of a special product in their community. Others celebrate the history or the habits of the community.

Festivals of this kind are likely to change from year to year.   You may write the Chamber of Commerce of a community sponsoring a festival to learn of its plans for the coming year.

Here is a list of colorful celebrations known throughout the country:

Apple Blossom Festival — Wenatchee, Washington

Cotton Carnival — Memphis, Tennessee

Fiesta Day — Taos, New Mexico

Frontier Days — Cheyenne, Wyoming

Pumpkin Day — Eureka, Illinois

Rose Festival — Portland, Oregon

Tulip Time — Holland, Michigan

Watermelon Day — Rocky Ford, Colorado

Winter Carnival — St. Paul, Minnesota

Perhaps you know of other interesting celebrations to add to this list.

Plan a study of one or more of these days, following the suggestions on pages 171–175.   The next few pages in this unit will also help you.

# REPORTING ON A SPECIAL FESTIVAL

Jack lived in Wyoming, where Frontier Days is celebrated. This is a special festival of the cow country. Here is Jack's report:

## Frontier Days

In Cheyenne, Wyoming, we celebrate Frontier Days every July. One morning there is a parade about three miles long, with Indians and cowboys on ponies. One float shows Buffalo Bill shooting light bulbs out of the air, and he hits every time. There are about six bands.

In the afternoon, the real show takes place at the fairgrounds. Cowboys ride bucking horses, steers, and buffaloes. A cowboy must stay with his horse for ten seconds from the time the horse starts bucking. He must "scratch," or spur the horse, three times forward and "scratch" backward all the rest of the time. He is disqualified if he pulls leather, loses a stirrup, or is bucked off.

The most dangerous event of the show is the bulldogging contest. The man who wins this contest wins the day's money.

I. If you like Jack's report, tell why.

II. On the blackboard make an outline of the three main topics of his report. Under each main topic, list the subtopics you find in each paragraph.

# GIVING AN EXPLANATION

After Jack gave his report, Ann asked, "What is a bulldogging contest?" Here is Jack's explanation:

Two cowboys, called a hazer and a bulldogger, ride out on their trained ponies. They single out a steer they wish to throw. The hazer rides up beside the steer to keep him running straight. The bulldogger rides up on the other side of the animal.

At the right moment the bulldogger slides from his saddle and grabs the steer's horns. The weight of the bulldogger twists his neck and throws him to the ground.

The bulldogger who throws a steer in the shortest length of time wins the contest.

Was Jack's explanation clear? Did he make you see just what takes place in a bulldogging contest? Did he tell the steps in the right order?

When you give an explanation, try to meet the following standards.

---

### STANDARDS FOR AN EXPLANATION

1. If possible, tell the steps in the order in which they happen.
2. Stick to the subject.
3. Be brief, accurate, and clear.
4. Use words that make pictures.

---

## Practice with Explanations

Give a brief explanation in answer to one of these questions:

1. What makes a helicopter fly?
2. Why do we celebrate Independence Day?
3. How do you make lemonade?
4. How do you pitch a curve?
5. What makes the wind blow?
6. How do you use a catalogue?
7. What is the best way to bathe a puppy?
8. How do you pick peaches, apples, or cherries?
9. How are clouds formed?
10. How is it possible for a bear to sleep all winter and yet keep alive?

# PLANNING A FESTIVAL BOOK

Plan to make a class book about the interesting celebrations in different parts of our country. You can do this if each boy and girl will write his report. Then the reports may be bound together to make a festival book.

Read the report on the opposite page. Then answer these questions:

1. What do you like about Charles's report?
2. How many paragraphs has it? What is the main topic of each? Do the sentences in each paragraph stick to the topic?
3. Did Charles keep his sentences apart?
4. Does each sentence begin and end correctly?
5. What proper nouns did Charles use? Did he write them correctly?

When you write a report, meet these standards.

---

### STANDARDS FOR A WRITTEN REPORT

1. Make an outline of the main topics.
2. Plan a paragraph for each main topic. See that each sentence in the paragraph sticks to the topic.
3. Choose a good title for your report.

---

After you have written your report, check it by the questions on page 36.

# Mule Day in Columbia

Every year on the first Monday in April, Mule Day is celebrated in Columbia, Tennessee. People come from far and near to see the parade.

In the long parade there are many floats. There are mules, horses, and ponies with gaily-dressed girls and men riding them. Here and there are school bands.

The prettiest girl in Maury County is chosen queen of the festival. A number of judges choose the finest mule in the parade. When the parade reaches the courthouse, Miss Maury County crowns King Mule.

After the parade the children go to the stands and buy popcorn, candy, and cool drinks. The men go to the auction, where thousands of mules are sold.

Charles Long

# WRITING FOR INFORMATION

You may not find books that tell about the special festivals of the different sections of our country. If you wish to know about a festival listed on page 179, write a letter to the Chamber of Commerce of the town in which it is held. Use the letter of request on page 226 as a model for your letter.

The two important words in the name *Chamber of Commerce* must be written with capital letters. In writing the name of any club or organization, follow the rule for writing other proper names.

Since you are writing to an organization, use the greeting *Gentlemen*. Follow it with a colon.

If you wish to find out about a number of the festivals listed, plan one letter and ask someone to write it on the blackboard. Be sure to make the body of the letter brief and courteous.

Choose different girls and boys to write the letters, using the letter on the blackboard as a model. Each one should use the correct inside address for the town to which he is writing, and name the festival in which he is interested.

Each boy and girl should ask someone else to check his letter by the questions on page 229. Any corrections should be made very neatly.

Plan together the correct form for addressing the envelopes for your letters. Use the one on page 228 as a model.

# MORE VERB FORMS

In your reports on holidays and festivals, you may tell about people who sing and bells that ring. Do you use the verbs *sing* and *ring* correctly? Study these forms:

| *Present Time* | *Past Time* | *With a Helper* |
|---|---|---|
| sing | sang | have sung |
| ring | rang | was rung |

Read the following sentences aloud, listening to the underlined verbs:

1. The dancing children sang gay songs.
2. The waifs had sung carols all evening.
3. The bell rang out merrily to proclaim freedom.
4. On New Year's Eve the bells had rung out from the towers.

## Practice

Read each sentence aloud and put in the correct verb form:

1. The engineer had (rang, rung) the bell.
2. Who (rang, rung) the bell for recess?
3. The chimes were (rung, rang) on Christmas Eve.
4. We (sang, sung) five carols in the assembly.
5. Have you ever (sang, sung) "Noël"?
6. The room (rang, rung) with merriment.
7. Our national song is (sang, sung) at every assembly.

[ 187 ]

# MAKING YOUR BOOKLET

Choose a committee of editors to read and check the written reports prepared by the class. If a report needs correction or rewriting, the committee should return it to the writer and suggest what he is to do.

Choose another committee to make up your festival booklet. This committee should arrange the reports in order and prepare a table of contents. They might ask other boys and girls to draw or paint pictures for some of the reports. Still others may write poems.

The class may wish to plan the title and picture for the cover. Ask one or two persons who can draw and print well to prepare it.

When the book is completed, put it in your class library. Then everyone in the class will have an opportunity to read all the reports.

### Reviewing Quotations

Write the following story, using quotation marks, punctuation, and capital letters correctly:

### A Christmas Legend

According to an old legend, the beasts in the stables converse on Christmas Eve in this manner:

Christ is born,  crows the cock
When?  asks the raven
The crow answers,  This night
Where, where  cries the ox
In Bethlehem,  the sheep softly bleats

# HOW WELL
## DO YOU REMEMBER?

If you make a mistake in a test, turn to page 190 and take the practice having the same number.

TEST I.   Write each sentence.   Put in *sang* or *sung*.

1. We have __?__ the national anthem.
2. Jane and Agnes __?__ in the assembly program.
3. Had you ever __?__ with Jane before?
4. Our canary __?__ loudly this morning.

TEST II.   Write each sentence.   Put in *rang* or *rung*.

1. The telephone has __?__ six times this morning.
2. Has the tardy bell __?__ yet?
3. I __?__ the bell, but no one came to the door.
4. The men came in when I __?__ the dinner bell.

# A HOLIDAY PROGRAM

Perhaps you can give an assembly program for the school.   Plan a holiday play, or a program of short plays.   Here are some books of holiday stories and poems that will give you material:

Olcott, Frances J., *Good Stories for Great Holidays*
Humphrey, Grace, *Stories of the World's Holidays*
Wickes, Frances G., *Happy Holidays*
Olcott, Virginia, *Holiday Plays for Home, School, and Settlement*
Harrington, Mildred P., *Our Holidays in Poetry*

PRACTICE I.   *A.*  Read the following:

| | |
|---|---|
| I *sang* | The class *has sung* |
| The bird *sang* | The song *was sung* |
| The class *sang* | A robin *had sung* |

Use a helping word with *sung*, not with *sang*.

*B.*  Use *sung* or *sang* correctly in each sentence:

1. Nancy has __?__ on the radio.
2. Joan __?__ the words of our school song.
3. Has Don ever __?__ in the choir?
4. They __?__ the chorus over and over again.

PRACTICE II.   *A.*  Be careful in choosing *rang* or *rung*.  Always use a helping word with *rung*.  Never use a helping word with *rang*.  Read the following:

> The bells *rang*      The chimes *have rung*

*B.*  Use *rang* or *rung* correctly in each sentence:

1. The church bells have __?__ all morning.
2. I was frightened when the fire bell __?__.
3. His voice __?__ out in the quiet room.
4. Has he __?__ down the curtain yet?

### Review Practice

1. Write each of the following sentences, putting in the correct word:

    1. Have the peaches (began, begun) to ripen?

    2. Has your brother ever (flew, flown) a plane?

3. Mark (began, begun) to swim across the pool.
4. Jerry (growed, grew) tired of waiting.
5. "Write to me often," Alice (says, said).
6. The maple trees have (grown, grew) faster than the elms.
7. The whistles were (blown, blowed) at noon.
8. Has the quarterback (thrown, threw) a pass yet?
9. I saw (a, an) elephant at the circus.
10. George Washington (threw, throwed) a coin across the river.
11. The wind (blowed, blew) my papers across the room.
12. On the lower branch perched (a, an) tiny oriole.

2. In each sentence there is either a contraction or a possessive noun with the apostrophe left out. Read the sentence carefully and find the word that needs an apostrophe.

Write each sentence and put in an apostrophe where it is needed.

1. Isnt Nancy ready to go?
2. We saw the boys hat blow off.
3. I havent seen Jerry for two days.
4. The puppies ears are long and silky.
5. The Dairymens Fair will be held soon.
6. Childrens Book Week is in November.

[ 191 ]

# Unit Six

## ORGANIZING A CLUB

## TALKING IT OVER

One morning Ray came to school, beaming. "I've just heard something I want to tell the class," he said to Miss Brown. "This morning, while I was at the filling station with Dad, a salesman drove in. He said our town was the best in the county."

"Did he tell you why he thought so?" asked Gerald.

"Yes, he did," replied Ray. "He said our streets are wide and clean, and because of the town circle there are never any traffic snarls. He said our factories are busy, our stores are up-to-date, and everyone is friendly. He told me I was lucky to live in such a fine town."

"We are, too," added Marion. "Some men came all the way from Washington, D. C., to visit our cheese factories."

"What about our high school band?" asked Stephen. "It has won state honors for the town."

"You're right about that, Stephen," said Gladys.

"In the summertime people come for many miles to hear the band concerts," said Tom.

"They come to see the Silver Falls along the river, too," put in Alec. "The falls are the highest in this part of the country, and they give us a great deal of electrical power."

"Yes," said Miss Brown. "The men who decided to build a town here used very good judgment. It is up to each one of us to help their dreams for our town to come true."

"Maybe our class can do something that will help keep our town on top," said Ray.

"We could form a club and help boost the town as the Chamber of Commerce does," said Allan.

"We could call it the Boosters Club," said Ann.

"That's a very good name," said Miss Brown. "Each of you can do many things to boost our town,

but by working as a club, you can accomplish much more than any one of you can alone."

## FORMING A CLUB

Would you like to organize your class into a club to boost your community? As a club, you could help others to appreciate the many fine things about your community. Perhaps you could also find ways to improve your community.

Talk over your plans with your teacher. Decide what the purpose of your club will be. Think of a name that states this purpose.

Every club must have a real reason for being, or it will not last long. Every member must support the club and do all he can to make it worth while. If your class is willing to work together, your club will be a success.

[ 195 ]

# ELECTING OFFICERS

You know that a club is made up of members and officers. The members elect officers to carry on the club business. A club needs at least three officers: a president, a vice-president, and a secretary.

The president of a club acts as chairman at club meetings. The vice-president performs these duties when the president is absent. When electing these officers, choose boys or girls who are real leaders.

The secretary keeps a record of each meeting and writes all letters for the club. In electing a secretary, choose someone who writes sentences and paragraphs clearly and correctly.

A temporary chairman should be appointed by your teacher. A committee should prepare the ballots. The chairman will take charge of the elections until a president is elected.

After each member has written the name of his choice for president, two tellers, appointed by the chairman, may collect the ballots and tally the votes on the blackboard, as the children in the picture are doing. In some clubs the president and vice-president are elected separately. Others may decide on only one ballot, the one getting the most votes being elected president, and the one getting the second highest number of votes, vice-president.

Study the picture on page 196. Who will be president? Who will be vice-president? If there is a tie for first or second place, the members should vote again on the names that are tied.

The secretary is usually elected separately because a person who might make a good club president might not make a good secretary. Can you tell why?

I. If you have decided to form a club, you will need to elect officers. Ask your teacher to appoint a temporary chairman.

Decide how you will cast your votes. Why isn't it wise to vote for club officers by a show of hands?

Do not forget boys or girls who are absent. They may make very good officers.

II. Your secretary will need to make a roll for the club. Each member can help by writing his name plainly on a slip of paper, with the last name first.

The secretary should arrange the names in alphabetical order and write them in her club notebook so that she may call the roll at each meeting.

# HOLDING A CLUB MEETING

There are certain rules for conducting a meeting. When everyone follows these rules, the meeting proceeds according to the plan that the officers have worked out.

The dialogue below shows how the Boosters conducted their first meeting. Notice how the president opened the meeting. When did the secretary call the roll? How did the members address the president before taking part in the meeting?

*President* (*rising and waiting for attention*). The meeting will now come to order. The secretary will call the roll. (*Secretary calls roll.*)

*President.* The subject of our first program is "Why We Like Our School." The secretary will announce each number on the program.

*Secretary* (*rising*). The first number on our program is "School Days," to be sung by everyone present. (*All stand and sing.*)

The second number is by Miss Wade, our principal, who took time out of a busy day to talk to us.

*Miss Wade* (*rising*). Mr. President and members of the Boosters Club: I am very much interested in your club. It is always good to find out things about our school and town. It is fine, too, to try to improve them both. Please come to me whenever I can help your club in any way. Thank you for inviting me in to your first meeting.

[ 198 ]

*President.* Thank you, Miss Wade. The Boosters Club appreciates your support.

*Secretary.* Our next number is a talk by George Frey on "Safety on the Playground."

*George.* Mr. President and fellow members: (*George gives his talk. After being introduced by the secretary, the rest of the members on the program address the president and give their talks.*)

*President.* That closes our program. Before the meeting is adjourned (ă·jûrnd′), I should like to appoint Ann Blair as chairman of the program committee. For the next month Ann and her committee will plan the programs for the club. They will also post the date of each club meeting. The meeting is now adjourned.

I. Did the president keep the meeting running smoothly? What appointment did he make? How did he close the meeting?

II. In what ways did the secretary help the president?

III. Chairmen of most committees are usually appointed by the president instead of being elected by the club. Can you tell why?

IV. You have just read each of the following expressions. Are you sure what each one means?

> come to order
> number on the program
> chairman of the program committee
> meeting adjourned

If you use these terms whenever you conduct a club meeting, you will soon become familiar with them.

## WRITING THE MINUTES

A club secretary keeps a record of each meeting. This record is called the *minutes*. During the meeting, the secretary takes notes. After the meeting, she writes the minutes in final form for the club's records.

At each meeting the minutes of the previous meeting are read and approved. If there are any mistakes or omissions, the members may suggest corrections.

[ 200 ]

Study these minutes. They were written by the secretary of the Boosters Club.

November 12, 19—

The first meeting of the Boosters Club was held in the Fifth Grade classroom, Friday, November 12, at three o'clock. President Dave Held presided. All members were present.
The following program was given:

Why We Like Our School

School Days — a song.......Club members
Talk.........................Miss Wade
Safety on the Playground.....George Frey
Keeping Our School Grounds
   Neat......................Mary Tarp
The Story of Our School.......Lon Berry

After the program, President Held announced that Ann Blair had been appointed chairman of the program committee for one month.

*Emma Fuller*, Secretary

I. Are the time and place of the meeting given? Do the minutes tell who presided at the meeting? Are all the members on the program listed? What appointment was recorded? Why did Emma date and sign the minutes?

II. Did Emma begin and end all sentences properly? Did she indent all paragraphs?

[ 201 ]

# CHOOSING COMMITTEES

Think over the different activities of your club. At a club meeting, discuss the committees you will need to carry on the work of your club.

After you have decided what committees you need, the officers and the teacher may appoint the chairman and the members for each. To help them choose, you may write on a slip of paper your name and the names of the committees on which you would enjoy working.

# WORKING ON COMMITTEES

A committee must work as a team. When you are appointed to a committee, check your work by these standards.

---

### STANDARDS FOR COMMITTEE WORKERS

1. Know what your work is.
2. Do your part to make discussions helpful.
3. Do cheerfully whatever is asked of you.
4. Present any suggestions you may have to your chairman.
5. Pull together with your committee at all times.

---

If each member of your committee measures himself by these standards, you will accomplish a great deal of work.

# PLANNING COMMITTEE WORK

The Boosters Club had a health committee. It was the work of this committee to learn about the health ·services of the community and report the information to the members of the club.

The committee met with Miss Brown to plan their work. First, they drew up this chart to work by:

| Health Services | How We Can Learn about Them |
|---|---|
| County Clinic | Visit |
| City Health Officer | Send list of questions |
| School Nurse | Invite to speak |
| Local Doctor | Interview |

Together they drew up a list of questions to send to the City Health Officer. They also worked out a set of questions to ask a local doctor.

Then they divided the rest of the work. Using the committee's questions, Frank wrote and mailed a letter to the City Health Officer. Amy called upon a local doctor and asked the questions the committee had prepared. She took careful notes on what the doctor told her.

Wayne, the chairman of the committee, telephoned the school nurse and the county clinic. The school nurse agreed to talk to the club on any health subject they chose. The superintendent of the clinic invited the club and Miss Brown to visit the clinic as his guests some Saturday morning. Wayne thanked the superintendent and said he would deliver the message.

# PRESENTING A COMMITTEE REPORT

As soon as they had gathered their information, the health committee met again to plan their report. They decided that Frank could read to the club the letter he received from the Health Officer. From the notes Amy took on her conversation with the doctor, they made a short play, or skit.

Then they listed the topics in their report in this way:

Health Committee Report

1. Introduction .. Wayne White, Chairman
2. Hints from a Health
   Officer.................Frank Grant
3. The Doctor Says —(a skit)...Bob West
   Amy Bryant
4. A Double Surprise.......Wayne White

I. Sometimes the chairman presents the report of his committee. The health committee felt that their report would be more interesting if all the members took part. Do you think they were right?

II. The committee decided that their chairman should open and close their report. Why was this a good plan? Why did they place the news about the school nurse and the clinic at the end of their report?

III. Do you like the different ways in which the committee decided to present their report? Discuss with your classmates other interesting ways to present committee reports.

# SPEAKING CORRECTLY

In giving reports of any kind, it is important to pronounce all your words correctly.

1. Some boys and girls drop letters within words. Notice the underlined letter within each of these words. Say the word correctly.

| | | | |
|---|---|---|---|
| strength | wanted | surprise | gentle |
| pumpkin | government | temporary | secretary |

2. Are you careful to say words ending in "ture" correctly? Pronounce each of these words. Do not end the word with "er."

picture     nature          posture          moisture

## Check Test 7: Correct Forms

1. Write each sentence, using the right form:
    1. We (knew, knowed) the rules.
    2. (Don't, Doesn't) he want to go?
    3. I have (known, knew) her a long time.
    4. It (doesn't, don't) matter.

2. Do you always use *learn* and *teach* correctly? Write these sentences. Put in the right form.
    1. I __?__ my dog a new trick every day.
    2. Did you __?__ your part quickly?
    3. If you __?__ me, I can __?__ to play tennis.

If you make any mistakes, turn to page 284 for further help.

## COURTESY TO A SPEAKER

Before the school nurse came to talk to the Boosters Club about good health habits, the members drew up a list of questions they wished to ask her. They also helped the president work out this introduction:

Fellow Boosters, most of you already know Miss Meadows, our school nurse. through the good work she is doing at our school. Today she will talk to us about good health habits. Afterward, she will answer our questions. Miss Meadows.

While Miss Meadows talked, the club members gave her their whole attention. After her talk, they asked the questions they had prepared. When the question period was over, the president said:

Thank you, Miss Meadows, for your fine talk and your helpful answers.

I. Do you think Miss Meadows felt that her time with the Boosters was well spent? Were the president's introduction and his "thank-you" speech courteous and sincere? In what ways were the club members courteous and helpful to the speaker?

II. Draw up a list of questions to ask a speaker you have invited to address your club. Such questions will tell him what you wish to know.

III. Plan an introduction and a "thank-you" speech. Use the speeches on page 206 as models, but fit your speeches to your own speaker.

## Practice with Correct Forms

Are you always careful to use correct forms of words when you make speeches? Read these sentences. Choose the right forms.

1. "The meeting has come to order," (said, says) Bob.
2. The meeting had (began, begun) on time.
3. Our club has (growed, grown) a great deal.
4. The principal made (a, an) address.
5. Our speaker has (flew, flown) over China.
6. Have you (sang, sung) the new club song?
7. The bugler (blowed, blew) his horn for us.
8. We have (threw, thrown) off our coats.
9. When the bell has (rang, rung), the meeting will adjourn.
10. We (sang, sung) our favorite hymn.

# MAKING A MOTION

At one meeting of the Boosters Club, Tom started this club discussion:

*Tom.* Mr. President.

*President.* Tom.

*Tom.* By listening to the different committee reports, we have learned a lot about our community. Can we use this information to boost our town?

*President.* That's a good question, Tom. How does the rest of the club feel about the matter?

*Marion (rising).* Mr. President.

*President.* Marion.

*Marion.* I think Tom is right. If we're going to live up to our name, we ought to boost our town.

*Bob.* Mr. President.

*President.* Bob.

*Bob.* Last summer, on my trip West, I collected folders of some towns we visited. I make a motion that we put our information into a folder.

*President.* A motion has been made that the club make a folder. Is there a second to the motion?

*Guy (rising).* Mr. President, I second the motion.

*President.* The motion has been seconded. Is there any discussion?

*Mary (rising).* Mr. President, I know where we can get pictures of the Falls for the cover.

*President.* Thank you, Mary. Is there any other

discussion? (*After a pause*) All in favor of Bob's proposal raise your right hand. (*Most of the club raise their right hands.*) The motion is carried.

Tom started the discussion with his question. But Bob made the motion when he said, "*I make a motion that we put our information into a folder.*" Until someone puts the matter under discussion into a motion and another person seconds it, no vote can be taken. Who seconded Bob's motion?

After a motion is made and seconded, the president calls for discussion. When did the president call for a vote?

Motions are often voted on by a show of hands rather than by a written ballot. Can you tell why? A majority, or over half, of a group usually carries a motion. If less than half of the club had raised their hands, would the motion have carried?

### Practice

Here is a list of suggested activities that one club drew up. Read over the list carefully. Then be ready to put each suggestion in the form of a motion. Remember to say, "I make a motion that . . . ." or "I move that . . . ."

1. Planning an Easter Egg roll
2. Inviting mothers to a Mother's Day party.
3. Making a class booklet.

Be ready also to second motions that any of your classmates may make.

[ 209 ]

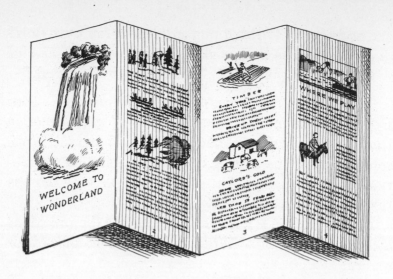

## MAKING A COMMUNITY FOLDER

Bob brought his collection of folders to the next meeting of the club. After looking them over, the members decided that more than one committee were needed to make a folder. So they chose an editorial committee, an art committee, and a production committee and divided the work among them.

The editorial committee read the information the club members had gathered about the community and wrote short articles. The art committee found or drew pictures and maps. The production committee found paper for the folders and made plans to print the written material and pictures prepared by the other two committees.

After the three committees were appointed, the committee chairmen and Miss Brown decided on the size and shape of the folder and made an outline of what it would contain.

This was the outline Miss Brown and the committee chairmen made:

Page 1.   Cover.   Welcome to Wonderland
          Picture of Silver Falls
Page 2.   How We Grew (history)
          Sketches
Page 3.   Why We Grew (lumber and dairies)
          Pictures or sketches, graphs
Page 4.   Where We Play (parks, forest reserves)
          Pictures
Page 5.   Why We're Healthy (health services)
          Charts
Page 6.   All Together (schools, churches, etc.)
          Sketches
Page 7.   Highways and Byways
Page 8.   Back.   Map of community

When the Boosters were sure of the number of the pages of their folder, they made a layout, or plan, for each page.

At the top of page 210 you will see the layouts for the first four pages of the Boosters' folder.

The layout of a page shows where the title will be. It shows what the picture will be and where it will be placed on the page. It also shows how much space will be left for written material.

The layouts helped all the committees to see and check their part of the work.

[ 211 ]

# MAKING THE FOLDER

With the help of Miss Brown, the production committee found enough paper to make thirty folders. They cut the paper to the right size and made arrangements to use the school duplicating machine.

At the same time, the art committee was gathering pictures and making maps and sketches. The art teacher helped them cut the sketches on stencils and run them on the duplicating machine.

The editorial committee checked with the art committee about the amount of space the sketches would take. Then they fitted their articles to the space left on each page. The members of the committee checked the work of each other to be sure that every word, every sentence, and every paragraph in the articles were right.

The work of the production committee really began when the art and editorial committees turned their work over to them. They had to typewrite all the articles on stencils and run them off on the duplicating machine.

The editorial committee helped to fold and staple the folders, and the art committee pasted a print of Silver Falls on each folder.

When the finished folders were turned over to the president of the Boosters Club, all three committees were proud of their work.

On the opposite page you will see two pages from the Boosters' folder.

The first white man to settle
in Silver Creek County was John
Gaylord. In 1849, he came down
Silver Creek in a canoe. He set
up headquarters in a hollow tree
and made a treaty with the Indians.

When John Gaylord's friends
heard of the land he had discovered, they followed him in boats.
In 1853, they named their town
after him.

In 1890, the town of Gaylord
was wiped out by a forest fire.
The people chose a better site
and laid out their new town in
the form of a wagon wheel. The
hub of the wheel was the center
of town; the spokes were the
streets.

In this way Gaylord could grow
in all directions. It has never
again been hemmed in by fire.

Visit the City Museum at 60
High Street today. You can still
see John Gaylord's first home
there.

T-i-m-b-e-r!

Every year loggers cut mil-
lions of feet of timber from
our forest storehouse. Mills
along Silver Creek make the timber into many useful things.

Drive up the Silver Creek
Highway and watch our lumberjacks and log jockeys at work.

Gaylord's "Gold"

Some visitors call the Gaylord cheese factories "mints"
because they turn out golden
bricks of cheese.

Less than 50 years ago, the
first cows were driven into the
Silver Creek Valley by a Swiss
farmer, who knew the secret of
cheese-making.

Today there are many cheese
factories in Gaylord. You can
visit them and see how the tasty
golden bricks are made.

## Reviewing Capital Letters

1. In preparing the folder (page 213), did the editorial committee use capital letters correctly? Find examples of each of these uses of capital letters:

    1. Name of a building
    2. First word in a sentence
    3. Name of a highway
    4. Name of a town
    5. Name of a person
    6. Name of a street
    7. Name of a valley
    8. Important words in a title

2. Check your knowledge of capital letters by filling in these blanks on a sheet of paper:

    1. My address is __?__.
    2. My parents' names are __?__.
    3. The name of my school is __?__.
    4. My birthday is __?__.
    5. On my last birthday __?__ was __?__ years old.
    6. The national anthem is "__?__."
    7. My favorite book is "__?__." It was written by __?__.
    8. My favorite song is "__?__."
    9. Patrick Henry said, "__?__ me liberty or give me death."

3. Ask a classmate to check your paper. After you have corrected your mistakes, copy the sentences in your Language Notebook.

# CORRECT VERB FORMS

In club discussions, do you always use the correct form of the verb? Study these forms carefully:

| Present Time | Past Time | With a Helper |
|---|---|---|
| speak | spoke | has spoken |
| break | broke | had broken |
| take | took | have taken |

Write each of the following sentences, putting in the correct form. Look at the lists above for help.

### Spoke or Spoken?

1. Mary __?__ politely to the visitors.
2. Has she __?__ to them before?
3. I have __?__ to Dad about it.
4. Dave __?__ before the class yesterday.

### Broke or Broken?

1. I __?__ the plane model last week.
2. Have you __?__ your new train?
3. The chair __?__ with a crash.
4. Tom has __?__ Mother's plate.

### Took or Taken?

1. Have you __?__ a book from the library?
2. We all __?__ one piece of candy.
3. Has the cat __?__ the catnip yet?
4. We __?__ a picnic lunch to the park.

# GIVING A CLUB SKIT

The Boosters Club was invited to give a ten-minute play, or skit, on a school program.

The club decided to use the legend of Rip Van Winkle as the model for their skit. A pioneer of their community would return to the world of today. In visiting his old haunts, he would meet two members of the Boosters Club.

The president appointed a committee to write the script for the skit and another to provide costumes and scenery.

The script committee wrote the dialogue so that it could be acted within ten minutes. Their title page looked like this:

Always a Booster

Time: Present
Place: Our Town
Cast:
Pioneer
First Booster (boy)
Second Booster (girl)

Then the committee read the skit to the club for suggestions. Copies of the corrected skit were given to the costume committee and to members of the club who wanted to try out for any of the three parts.

Tryouts were held during a club meeting, and the members chose the cast for the skit.

They judged the actors by the standards on the opposite page.

A few days before the program, the cast gave a performance of the skit before the club in order to get last-minute suggestions.

I. Do you think the skit was a success? Did it probably keep within the time provided for it?

II. Think of a legend or a story on which your club can base a skit. Then write the skit. Be sure to think of a good title. Keep it short.

---

### STANDARDS FOR ACTORS

1. Know your lines well.
2. Try to *be* the character you are acting.
3. Pick up your lines quickly.
4. Move naturally about the stage.
5. Try to keep your face toward the audience.
6. Speak loudly enough to be heard by all.

---

# HOW WELL
# DO YOU REMEMBER?

Take these tests to find out how well you remember what you learned in this unit.   If you make a mistake, take the practice bearing the same number.

TEST I.   Copy these sentences.   Use capital letters where they are needed.

1. My name is david jones.
2. I live at 105 elm street in norwood, maryland.
3. I was born in july.
4. I am a member of the camera club.

TEST II.   Choose the right form in each sentence:

1. We (spoke, have spoke) to the chairman.
2. Dave has (broke, broken) his bicycle.
3. They (took, have took) our pictures.
4. I have (broke, broken) Mother's jelly dish.
5. Have you (spoke, spoken) at the meeting?

## IF YOU NEED HELP

PRACTICE I.   *A.* Review the use of capital letters on pages 274–275.

*B.* Copy these sentences correctly:

1. I live in black lake, idaho.
2. My birthday comes on the fourth of july.
3. My father's name is dr. r. b. roberts.
4. My favorite song is "marching along."

PRACTICE II. *A.* Study the different forms of *take*, *break*, and *speak* given on page 215.

*B.* Choose the correct form in each of the following sentences:

1. I have (taken, took) my lunch all winter.
2. Have you (broke, broken) the doll carriage?
3. Speak when you are (spoken, spoke) to.
4. Ned has (taken, took) pictures of the club.
5. They (broke, have broke) open the piggy bank.
6. Had they (spoke, spoken) the truth?
7. I (had took, took) the book home.

## USING NEW EXPRESSIONS

In this unit you learned to use these expressions in conducting your club business:

committee chairman     all in favor
meeting adjourned     make a motion
come to order     motion is carried

I. Thumb through the unit and find other such expressions. List them on the blackboard. Then each of you may make up a sentence using one of these new terms correctly.

The other members of the class should listen to your sentence and tell you whether you have used the expression correctly.

II. Your teacher will appoint a temporary chairman of a meeting. Take turns making or seconding a motion, or taking part in the discussion.

[ 219 ]

# Unit Seven

## WRITING LETTERS

### A LETTER FROM CHINA

One day Tim brought a letter to school. It was from his uncle in China. When Tim put the envelope on the bulletin board, all the children gathered around to see the air-mail stamp that had brought it across the Pacific Ocean.

"Won't you read us your letter?" asked Joan.

"Yes, Tim," smiled Miss Graham. "We would all like to hear the interesting things your uncle has to say about China."

Tim skipped the parts of the letter that asked about his family and read only the parts about China.

"What a wonderful letter," said all the children. "Thank you for reading it to us."

"It was like taking a trip to China," said Bruce. "I could almost see the water buffalo and the rice paddies."

"I liked the Chinese words he used," said Bob. "It's fun learning words from other lands."

"The best parts of the letter are the pictures my uncle drew," said Tim. He passed the letter around so that everyone could see the clever drawings.

"Writing a letter is a wonderful way of sharing with others what we see, isn't it?" asked Beth.

"All letters don't do the same thing," Miss Graham told the children. "Tim's uncle wanted to have a chat with Tim. So he wrote him a *friendly* or *social* letter. What kind of letter would Tim's uncle write if he wanted to order a camera or ask a favor of an American businessman?"

"He would write a *business letter*," said Bruce. "My father helped me write a business letter when I ordered my new catcher's mitt from the sport catalogue."

"Did we write a business letter when we asked the city librarian to send us books of folk tales?" asked Margaret.

"Yes, Margaret," Miss Graham said. "Some business letters, like Bruce's, place orders. Others, like yours, ask favors of business people. Any letter addressed to a business person is a business letter. We shall soon learn some of the rules for writing good business letters."

"Any letter addressed to a friend is a friendly letter, isn't it?" asked Bob.

"Yes," agreed Miss Graham. "Most of the letters you write are friendly ones."

[ 222 ]

"All friendly letters aren't alike, though," said Ann. "Some are newsy and full of fun, like Tim's letter from his uncle in China. But others do just one thing, such as inviting us to a picnic and party."

"When Mary couldn't come to my party, she wrote me a letter saying she was sorry that she couldn't come," said Diana.

"When my brother won first prize in a contest, he received letters from his friends. They told him how happy they were for him," added Dave.

"I always write my grandparents a 'thank-you' letter at Christmas time," said Sally.

"You can make an apology by letter, too," grinned Bob. "I did when I painted our neighbors' fence by mistake."

All the children laughed at Bob's mistake.

"Well," smiled Miss Graham, "you seem to know a great deal about friendly letters already."

"We know that all letters should be courteous, no matter whether they are business or friendly letters," piped up Tom.

"All letters must be stamped and addressed correctly, too, or the postman won't be able to deliver them," put in Eileen.

"The post office does other things besides delivering letters," said Joan. "Yesterday I went with my mother to send a package to a friend of ours who lives in Greece."

"You can buy postal notes at the post office," said Bruce. "I bought one and sent it along with my letter to pay for my catcher's mitt."

"Why don't we visit the post office and see for ourselves what they do?" suggested Aaron.

"That's a very good idea, Aaron," said Miss Graham.

"Let's write the postmaster a letter," cried Dick, "and ask him when we may come."

"My father is a clerk at the post office," spoke up Mary. "He told me the postmaster likes people to visit him at the post office. He likes to show them our fine new post office."

# PAPER FOR LETTER WRITING

The next time you visit a stationery store, look at the many different sizes and colors of writing papers. Each of these papers has a special use.

Perhaps at home you have a little box of colored stationery with squirrels or chipmunks running down each sheet. Such paper is good for friendly letters. Can you tell why it is not suitable for business letters?

Plain white paper is more formal and dignified than colored paper. Most business people write their letters on sheets of white paper measuring about $8\frac{1}{2}$ by 11 inches. On a sheet of this size you can write all the parts of a business letter without crowding them. It also allows for wide margins, which make a letter attractive and easy to read.

A business envelope should always match the paper in color.

# A LETTER OF REQUEST

This is the letter the class sent to the postmaster.

```
                          Maywood Public School
                          Maywood, California
                          March 14, 19--


     Mr. Ray Mathews, Postmaster
     Maywood Post Office
     6 Center Street
     Maywood 2, California


     Dear Mr. Mathews:

        Our class is interested in learning

     how mail is handled in our city.  May

     we visit the post office some day next

     week and see for ourselves?

        Thank you for whatever help you can

     give us.

                          Very truly yours,

                          The Fifth Grade
```

I. The *heading* of a business letter is like the heading of some friendly letters. A business letter, however, has an *inside address*, which is the same as the address on the envelope. Find the inside address in the letter above.

[ 226 ]

How is Mr. Mathews' title separated from his name? Find the zone number. How is it separated from the state?

II. Find the *greeting* in the letter. When you write to a business house and do not address a particular person, use *Gentlemen* as the greeting; or you may use *Dear Sir* or *Dear Madam* if you are writing to one man or woman. A colon follows the greeting of a business letter.

III. Is the *body* of the class's letter brief, clear, and courteous?

IV. Notice the *closing* and the *signature* of the letter. What punctuation follows the closing?

V. Are the paragraphs of the letter indented? Notice the left-hand margins in the heading, the inside address, and the body of the letter. A business house usually leaves margins of one inch or more on all sides of a business letter.

VI. How many capital letters can you find in the letter? Tell why each is used. Where is each comma used and why? Where are periods used?

VII. If your letter is as courteous and attractive as the one opposite, it is likely to receive a favorable reply.

Before you mail your letter, be sure to proofread it for words you have omitted or misspelled. Make your handwriting neat and readable.

# ADDRESSING AN ENVELOPE

This is the model of the envelope that Miss Graham's class worked out on the blackboard.

```
Fifth Grade
Maywood School
Maywood, California


                  Mr. Ray Mathews, Postmaster

                  Maywood Post Office

                  6 Center Street

                  Maywood 2, California
```

I. Find the *receiver's address*. Is it the same as the inside address in the letter on page 226? Why is it important to have this part correct?

II. Notice where the *return address* is placed. Why is the return address necessary?

III. Only stamped letters are delivered. How much postage is needed to send the letter?

## WORDS THAT SOUND ALIKE

If you do not know the difference between these pairs of words, look them up in your dictionary. Then use each one in a sentence.

week weak    mail male    tail tale    some sum

# CHECKING BUSINESS LETTERS

It is a good idea to make a rough copy of a business letter before you prepare it for mailing. Then judge it by the following standards.

---

### STANDARDS FOR BUSINESS LETTERS

1. State the purpose of the letter briefly and courteously in the first paragraph.
2. Use short, clear sentences.
3. Make a separate paragraph for each topic.
4. Use a businesslike greeting and closing.
5. Use good business stationery.
6. Keep a copy of the letter.

---

After you are sure that the body of your letter meets these standards, check the entire letter by the following questions:

1. Does the heading include the place and date?
2. Is the inside address correct?
3. Are paragraphs indented properly?
4. Are all words and names spelled correctly?
5. Are all margins neat and even?
6. Are capital letters and punctuation marks used correctly in all parts of the letter?
7. Is the handwriting easy to read?
8. Is the letter free of smudges?

After you have given the rough copy of your letter this double check, copy it for mailing.

## Practice with Business Letters

1. Copy this letter. Supply missing capital letters, punctuation marks, and signature. Use the letter on page 226 as a model.

```
                          834 elm street
                          auburn maine
                          april 6 19—
miss helen trent
auburn public library
auburn maine

dear miss trent

   our class is studying about the post
offices of other days. Do you have
books that would help us?
   thank you for any help you can give.

                  very truly yours
```

2. Write a business letter, requesting permission to visit a newspaper or other place of business in your community. Be sure to direct your letter to the person in charge. Check the spelling of his name and address in the telephone directory. Give your letter the double check provided on page 229.

3. Draw an envelope for the letter. Address it properly. Check the receiver's address with the inside address of your letter. Is your own return address properly placed?

4. Give your letter and your envelope to a classmate to check. Be sure to correct any mistakes that he marks. Then put the corrected models in your Language Notebook.

## Reviewing Singular and Plural Nouns

You know that a noun always names one or more than one. Read these sentences:

1. I wrote a *letter* to my *friend*.
2. Dave wrote *letters* to his *friends*.

Find the singular nouns in sentence 1. Find the plural nouns in sentence 2.

You have learned that most nouns form their plurals by adding *s* to their singular forms, such as: clerk, clerk*s*; package, package*s*. Some nouns add *es* to the singular, such as: dish, dish*es*.

A few nouns change *f* to *v* before adding *es*, such as: shel*f*, shel*ves*. Other nouns change *y* to *i* before adding *es*, such as: fly, fl*ies*.

Some nouns make changes within the word, such as: m*a*n, m*e*n. Others add extra letters, such as: child, child*ren*. A few nouns such as *deer* do not change at all.

## Practice with Plurals

Write the plural of each of these words and use it in a sentence. If you are not sure how to spell the plural, use your dictionary.

| | | | |
|---|---|---|---|
| bicycle | stamp | match | foot |
| glass | knife | lady | trout |
| mouse | cry | postman | leaf |

# A TRIP TO THE POST OFFICE

The children were pleased when Mr. Mathews called and invited them to visit the post office.

"What would you like to see first?" asked Mr. Mathews when Miss Graham and the children arrived.

"Show us what happens to our letters after the postman picks them up," said Glenn.

Mr. Mathews took the children into a busy room, where men were sorting letters.

"The postman dumps the letters on this table," said Mr. Mathews. "Poorly and improperly addressed letters are tossed aside. If they cannot be read and have no return addresses, they are sent to the Dead Letter Office."

"Now I see why the receiver's address and the return address are so important," said Bill.

"Properly addressed letters go through this machine," continued Mr. Mathews. "It marks the date and cancels the stamps."

Just then a mail truck backed up to the door.

"Here comes the afternoon mail from the East," said Mr. Mathews. "This same truck takes all our outgoing mail to the railroad station. On the train the mail is sorted by towns."

Then Mr. Mathews showed the children where to buy stamps and where to find air-mail schedules.

"Always mail a package at the post office," explained Mr. Mathews as he took the children to the parcel-post department. "We tell you how much postage it needs."

"Can we send money through the mail?" asked Tim.

"A postal note is the safest way to send small amounts," answered Mr. Mathews. He let the children watch a clerk make out a postal note.

After their post-office tour, the children thanked Mr. Mathews and his helpers.

"If you want to thank us," said Mr. Mathews, "always address your letters and packages correctly."

# GAVE AND GIVEN

Read these sentences:

1. The postman *gave* me a package.
2. *Have* you *given* me your new address?

Never use a helping word with *gave*. Always use a helping word with *given*. Write these sentences. Fill the blanks with *gave* or *given*.

1. Harvey has __?__ me his address.
2. The doctor __?__ us an interview.
3. Have you ever __?__ your dog a bath?
4. The class __?__ a postal pageant.
5. They have __?__ a good performance.

## Reviewing Correct Forms

In writing letters, do you use correct forms? Write these sentences. Use the right forms.

1. "We're all here," (says, said) Tharon.
2. Have you (begun, began) your letter?
3. I dreamed I had (flew, flown) to China.
4. The wind has (blowed, blown) all day.
5. I am copying (a, an) address.
6. Paul (threw, throwed) the ball to first.
7. Have you (sung, sang) in the choir before?
8. The bells have (rang, rung) for an hour.
9. Who has (spoke, spoken) to you?
10. Has Tom (took, taken) a shower?
11. My violin string is (broke, broken).
12. You have (growed, grown) a great deal.

# SIT AND SAT

Do you make mistakes with the verbs *sit* and *sat?*
*Sit* expresses present time. *Sat* expresses past
time. Sometimes you need to use a helping word
such as *has* or *have* with *sat.*

Notice the underlined verbs in these sentences:

1. I s̲i̲t̲ at my desk now.
2. I s̲a̲t̲ at my desk yesterday.
3. I h̲a̲v̲e̲ s̲a̲t̲ at my desk every day this week.

Read these sentences. After you are sure what the
sentence means, fill in each blank with *sit* or *sat:*

1. Where would you like to __?__?
2. We have __?__ near the door in the past.
3. The children like to __?__ in the front rows.
4. Dick __?__ down to watch the game.
5. Have they __?__ down yet?

## Practice with Nouns

1. Match these common nouns with proper nouns:

city    grade    teacher    country    library

List them as follows:

| *Common Nouns* | *Proper Nouns* |
| --- | --- |
| school | Westport School |

2. Which of these words should be written with
capital letters? Which, with small letters? Use
your dictionary if you are not sure.

brazil nut    indian    mexico    neptune

# READING A FRIENDLY LETTER

Here is a letter that made Ann happy all day.

> 62 Revere Avenue
> Bradford, Massachusetts
> April 3, 19—
>
> Dear Ann,
>
> Moving to New England is like stepping into a history book. Everywhere we go we think of the Pilgrims and Paul Revere.
>
> The country has many stone fences. The towns have tall, white churches.
>
> We are happy in my aunt's Cape Cod cottage. It has blue shutters and a blue roof.
>
> Won't it be wonderful if your family drives across the country to visit us?
>
> Love,
> Jane

I. Does Jane's letter tell about things of interest to Ann? Name words that would help Ann see New England.

II. Did Jane place all the parts of her letter correctly? Did she use capital letters and punctuation marks correctly? How many paragraphs did she use? Did she spell all words correctly?

## CHECKING FRIENDLY LETTERS

If your friendly letters meet all of these standards, your friends will enjoy them.

---

### STANDARDS FOR FRIENDLY LETTERS

1. Topics should be lively and interesting.
2. The writer should not talk about himself.
3. All questions asked by letter should be answered.
4. Action and picture words should be used.
5. Paper may be gay and colorful.

---

Use this set of questions to check your friendly letters for correctness:

1. Are all the parts in the right place?
2. Are spacings and margins even and neat?
3. Are all sentences complete?
4. Are all paragraphs properly indented?
5. Are capitals and punctuation marks used correctly?
6. Are all words spelled correctly?
7. Is the handwriting neat and readable?

If you can answer *Yes* to all these questions, your letter is ready to mail.

# IMPROVING SENTENCES

These sentences were taken from letters written by girls and boys. Improve them by breaking them into shorter sentences. Use capital letters and punctuation marks where they are needed.

1. I live in the country and I go to a community school and I ride the school bus every day.

2. I go for a walk with Grandfather every Saturday and sometimes we go to a movie and sometimes we visit my aunt.

3. Our class had a pet show and we invited our mothers and most of them came.

## Practice with Friendly Letters

1. Write to a friend or relative who lives in another part of the country. Describe to him how and where you live. Tell him what you do for fun. Use the letter on page 236 as a model.

Address an envelope for this letter. Use the one on page 228 as a model.

2. Do you have a "pen pal"? Some children get the names of other boys and girls from children's magazines or Sunday School papers. If you can find a "pen pal," write him a letter.

3. It is fun to set up a class post office. Elect a postmaster and an assistant. If each of you write a letter to your favorite book character, your postmaster will have interesting mail to collect.

# USING THE VERB *SET*

The verb *set* expresses the action *to put* or *to place* a thing somewhere.   Read the following sentences:

1. Please *set* the vase on the shelf.
2. Father *set* the clock.
3. The bowl of bulbs *was set* in a dark closet.

Never confuse *set* with *sit* or *sat*, which always refers to a position.

Read aloud each of these sentences.   Be sure to use the right word.

1. The cat (sits, sets) in the sun.
2. Will you (sit, set) the jar on the shelf?
3. We (sat, set) around the fire.
4. (Set, Sit) a saucer of milk on the floor.
5. Please (sit, set) very still.
6. I have been (sitting, setting) here a long time.

## Practice with Picture-Making Verbs

1. Write sentences using these verbs:

danced    jumped    whizzed    crawled    hopped

2. Think of a better verb to replace each of the underlined words in these sentences:

1. "Run for your lives!" said Bob.
2. Dick and Tom went to the fire.
3. After our hike we came home, too tired to move.
4. The trees moved in the wind.

[ 239 ]

## SENDING A PACKAGE

One class decided to surprise the shut-ins in a children's hospital with a package. The collecting committee gathered joke and picture books, cutouts, comics, puzzles, and games. The wrapping committee wrapped each present carefully. Then they wrapped the package securely.

The mailing committee made a label like this.

```
From:
Willow School
Racine, Wisconsin

          To: Miss Mary West, Superintendent
              The Children's Hospital
              Claremont, Wisconsin
```

Where is the receiver's address? the return address? Why are both necessary? How did the mailing committee know how much postage to put on the package?

# A "THANK-YOU" LETTER

A week later the class received this letter:

```
                        The Children's Hospital
                        Claremont, Wisconsin
                        May 5, 19—

Dear Fifth Grade,

    I cannot tell you how pleased the chil-
dren were with your package.  They are
still discovering surprises in your box.

    Thank you again for thinking of us.

                        Sincerely yours,

                        Mary West

                        Mary West,
                        for all the children
```

I. Read the words or sentences that make Miss West's letter sound sincere and grateful.

II. Why is Miss West's closing different from Jane's closing on page 236?

III. Did Miss West use capital letters and punctuation marks correctly?

IV. Has someone done you a favor or sent you a present lately?  If so, write a short "thank-you" letter.  Check your letter by the standards on page 237.

V. Draw a label for a package. Address it to someone you know.

# PLACING AN ORDER

One class formed a stamp club. At one of their meetings they decided to write for a packet of foreign stamps advertised in a children's magazine.

Below you can read the letter they wrote to order the stamps. It is signed by the president of the club.

1020 Westwood Drive
Denver, Colorado
March 4, 19—

La Jolla Stamp Company
Box 333 B
La Jolla, California

Gentlemen:

Our Stamp Club wishes to order one packet of the foreign stamps that you advertise for one dollar ($1.00).

Enclosed you will find a postal note for one dollar.

Please send the packet to me at the address given above.

Very truly yours,

*Bruce Price*

Bruce Price
President of the Stamp Club

I. An order letter should accurately describe the article ordered. It should mention the number of articles wanted, as well as the size and color if necessary. Find the sentence in the letter that describes what the club wanted.

II. An order letter should tell the cost of the article and where to send it. Does the club's letter do these two things?

If you order a catalogue or bulletin, it is courteous to enclose the necessary postage.

III. Turn to the standards and questions for business letters on page 229. Use them to check Bruce's letter. Do you find any mistakes?

### Practice with Order Letters

1. Think of an article you would like to order. Find in your telephone directory or newspaper the name and address of a firm selling this article.

2. Plan your letter carefully. Give a complete description of the article you want. List the number, size, price, or anything else that will help point out the article you have in mind. Tell how you will pay for the article and where you want it sent.

3. Using the letter on page 242 as a model, write a rough copy of your letter. Be sure you have all the necessary parts of a business letter. Check your letter by the standards and questions on page 229.

Ask a classmate to read your letter. Correct any mistakes he may find.

[ 243 ]

## WRITING A POSTAL CARD

When people are on trips or vacations, they often write brief messages on postal cards which they send to their families and friends.

Here is a postal card Dan received from Allan.

Crater Lake, Oregon

Dear Dan,
What fun we're having! Yesterday we saw cowboys. Today we are going to climb a mountain.
Your friend,
Allan

POST CARD

Dan Brown
158 Alder Drive
Denver, Colorado

I. Notice where Allan wrote his message. Why are all of his sentences short? Why are they placed together in one paragraph? Did Allan write anything he would mind anyone seeing?

II. Did Allan address the card correctly? Why is there no return address?

III. Allan did not date his card. How could Dan tell when it was mailed?

IV. If you have picture post cards at home, bring some of them to the class for display.

Get a penny postal from the post office and send a card to a friend or relative.

## DIVIDING WORDS

Read these sentences from Mary's letter:

Our class is having a party tomorrow afternoon. We are planning a Halloween celebration for the Fourth Grade.

The mark dividing *afternoon* and *celebration* is a *hyphen* (-). A hyphen is used when it is necessary to divide a word. Always break a word at the end of a syllable. Did Mary break the words *afternoon* and *celebration* at the right places? Consult your dictionary. Words of one syllable should not be broken.

On the blackboard show how you may divide the following words. Use your dictionary.

| morning | evening | midnight | dollar |
| elephant | cucumbers | nickel | buffalo |

## LEARNING NEW WORDS

In this unit you have learned several new words. Some are listed below.  If you are not sure of their meanings, look them up in your dictionary.

| | | | |
|---|---|---|---|
| apology | proofread | cancel | permission |
| stationery | receiver | packet | possession |
| superintendent | postmaster | receipt | sincere |

### Reviewing Kinds of Sentences

Read this paragraph from Dale's letter:

> When can we go skating, Old Timer?  I have a new pair of skates to break in.  What beauties they are!  Write me and let me know your plans.

How many kinds of sentences did Dale use?

Write a paragraph of your own.  Use at least one question, one sentence that shows surprise, and one that makes a statement.  Why are sentences that give commands not often used in letters?

Try to begin your sentences in as many different ways as possible.

## Reviewing Paragraphs

Using different kinds of sentences is one way to make your paragraphs more interesting to others.

A paragraph that sticks to the subject is also more interesting than one that does not.

I. Find the sentence in this paragraph that does not stick to the subject:

> All the children in our neighborhood skate on Howard's Pond. We take turns caring for the ice. We have picnics there in the summertime, too. Some of our parents come to watch us skate.

Now read the paragraph without that sentence. Don't you find the paragraph easier to understand?

A paragraph that does not tell things in order is also hard to read and understand.

II. Read this paragraph. Find the sentence that is out of order.

> When I plan to go skating, I dress warmly. As soon as I arrive at the pond, I put on my skates. I see that my skates are sharp before I go. Then I find my friends, and the fun begins.

Now read the paragraph again, putting this sentence in the right place. Do you find the paragraph easier to read now?

# A NOTE OF INVITATION

This is a note that Joe wrote to Dick, inviting him to spend a week end at the ranch:

```
                        Indian Head Ranch
                        R.F.D. #2
                        Spokane, Washington
                        March 8, 19—

Dear Dick,

    Dad and I hope your mother will let
you spend this week end with us on the
ranch.

    If you catch the bus that arrives in
Gem at six o'clock on Friday evening,
we shall meet you at the bus depot.

                        Your friend,

                        Joe
```

I.  Does Joe's invitation tell *who* is invited, to *what* he is invited, and *when* and *where* he is to come?

II.  What words or sentences would made Dick feel that Joe wanted him to come?

III.  What helpful directions did Joe give Dick?

IV.  Ask your mother whether you may invite a friend to go to the movies or have a picnic with you.  Write a note inviting your friend.  Be sure you give the necessary directions.

# ANSWERING INVITATIONS

This is the way Dick answered Joe's invitation to spend a week end at the Indian Head Ranch:

March 11, 19—

Dear Joe,

Thank you for the invitation to be a cowboy this coming week end.  I shall arrive at Gem on the six o'clock bus, as you suggested.

Until then,

*Dick*

Mary couldn't accept Jean's invitation to a picnic. This is the note she wrote:

April 8, 19—

Dear Jean,

I'm sorry I can't go on your picnic, but Grandmother is visiting us on that day.

Thank you for asking me.  I hope to hear all about your fun when I see you.

Love,

*Mary*

I. Imagine you have been invited to a wiener roast.  Write a short note, accepting the invitation.

II. Write a second note, telling why you cannot accept the same invitation.

## HOW WELL
## DO YOU REMEMBER?

If you make mistakes in any test, take the practice with the same number on page 251.

TEST I. Copy these parts of a letter, using capital letters and punctuation marks correctly:

> washington school
> elkhart, indiana
> april 3 19__

association of american railroads
928 transportation building
washington 6 d c

gentlemen

> very truly yours
> the fifth grade

TEST II. Use the correct word in each sentence:
1. We (sit, set) where we are told to.
2. (Sit, Set) the bucket down.
3. Goldilocks had (sat, set) in each chair.

TEST III. Use the correct word in each sentence:
1. Have you (gave, given) your talk?
2. He (gave, has gave) us the message.
3. We have (given, gave) the club yell.

TEST IV. Use the hyphen to show where you should break each of these words:

friendly    letter    envelope    request    gentlemen

[ 250 ]

PRACTICE I.  *A.*  On page 226 study the uses of capital letters and punctuation marks.

*B.*  Your teacher will dictate to you the letter on page 226.   Write it correctly.   Then check it against the model.

PRACTICE II.   *A.*  Study pages 235 and 239 for the uses of the verbs *sit, sat,* and *set.*

*B.*  Fill these blanks with the verbs *sit, sat,* or *set:*

    1.  The boys __?__ the model down carefully.
    2.  The bird __?__ in the tree, singing merrily.
    3.  Won't you __?__ here, please?
    4.  I have __?__ there before.

PRACTICE III.   *A.*  On page 234 read the lesson on *gave* and *given.*

*B.*  Write each of these sentences, using the right form of the verb:

    1.  Have you (given, gave) them their tickets?
    2.  I (gave, have gave) my rabbit some water.
    3.  James has (given, gave) a fine report.
    4.  Have you (gave, given) the correct address?

PRACTICE IV.   *A.*  Study the use of the hyphen on page 245.

*B.*  Use the hyphen to break each of these words properly:

inside    capital    madam    dictionary    syllable

# Unit Eight

## WRITING FOR FUN

## STORIES OF EVERYDAY LIFE

If someone were to ask you what type of story you like best, most of you would say, "I like to read about boys and girls of my own age." In other words, you like to read about good times that remind you of something that happened or could happen to you or to friends of yours.

One day, when the class planned to write stories of home experiences, Helen Grayson wrote a story that the class enjoyed very much. Though the event really occurred in her own home, she wrote about it as if it had happened to another group of people. Read her story.

### A Joke on Mother

"Homer, I've lost them again," Mrs. Pennywitt called out.

"Oh, Mother, not again!" answered Homer. "How could you lose your glasses again when I had just found them for you a half hour ago?"

"It was no trouble at all," replied Mrs. Pennywitt cheerily, shifting the roly-poly baby to the other arm. "It was really quite easy to do."

The twins wandered in. They shook their heads in reply to their mother's questioning look.

"We've looked everywhere — everywhere that you've ever left them before," said Hope, the girl twin.

"Think, Mother!" said the boy twin, Horace. "What have you been doing for the past half hour?"

"Not a thing really," protested Mrs. Pennywitt. "I just decided to write a letter to Uncle Joe; and when I looked for my glasses, they were gone."

She jerked her head away from the baby fingers that were trying to clutch at her face. "Don't, Virgie," she said.

"Did you make a grocery list, Mother?" asked Hope.

"No!" Mrs. Pennywitt's tone was positive.

"Or read the directions on a carton?" asked Homer.

"No!" Mrs. Pennywitt replied.

"Guh-guh!" gurgled Virgie, smiling up at his mother and reaching again for her face.

"Or use the telephone book?" suggested Horace.

"Oh, no!" Mrs. Pennywitt shook her head.

"Watch out!" yelled Homer, grabbing for the baby. "Virgie almost knocked your glasses off!"

He stopped short and stared at his mother.

"Oh, Mother!" he said accusingly.

"Oh, Mother!" cried Horace and Hope.

Mrs. Pennywitt put her hand to her eyes. She snatched off her glasses and looked at them in a dazed manner.

"Well!" she said. "Well, well!"

The children were doubled up with laughter. Soon Mrs. Pennywitt joined in. Virgie, not wanting to be left out of the fun, squealed happily.

"That's the best one on you yet, Mother," said Hope, gasping, and holding her sides.

"On me?" said Mrs. Pennywitt. "I would say, children, that it was a joke on all of us."

"All except Virgie," reminded Homer. "He's been grabbing at your glasses for the past ten minutes."

"That's right," said Hope. "Why, he even tried to say 'glasses,' didn't you, Virgie?"

"Guh-guh," crowed Virgie.

I. As you read Helen's story, did it bring to your mind something that has happened in your own family? Would you say that Helen chose a simple, everyday event? Why is it better to choose such an event for a story?

II. What do you like about the way Helen told her story? Do the characters in it seem natural? Do they speak as members of any family might speak at home?

III. Did Helen use conversation in her story? How did that help to give life to her story?

IV. Begin to think of amusing or exciting events that have taken place in your home lately. In the next few days, decide which one of them could be used as the subject of a good story. Then be ready to write a story in your next story-writing period in class.

You need not use your family name if you do not wish to. You may give the characters other names, as Helen did.

The lessons on the next three pages will help you to write your story correctly.

## Practice with Quotations

Before you write your story, review what you have learned about quotation marks. Then copy the following conversation, putting in quotation marks and other necessary punctuation:

A loud knocking lifted Tom from the midst of the spy-ring story he was reading. There before him in the doorway of the barn stood a rough-looking individual.

Trying to cover his fear with a weak smile, Tom said, Good morning.

Where are the papers growled the man.

Wh-wh-what papers stuttered Tom.

The papers in your cellar said the man.

But they aren't in the cellar protested Tom, still living in the world of the story.

Why, your mother called me and told me to come for two crates of old papers in the cellar exclaimed the man.

Oh — oh yes I'll take you to the cellar said Tom, coming back to real life.

# A NEW USE FOR COMMAS

Read the following sentences and notice the use of commas:

1. Homer, I've lost them again.
2. Did you make a grocery list, Mother?
3. I would say, children, that it was a joke on all of us.

To whom is sentence 1 addressed? sentence 2? sentence 3?

When the name of the person addressed appears in a sentence, it should be separated from the rest of the sentence by one or more commas.

In sentence 1, the name appears first and the comma follows it.

In sentence 2, where does the name of the person addressed appear? Where is the comma placed?

In sentence 3, the name of the persons addressed is in the middle of the sentence. How many commas separate it from the rest of the sentence?

### Practice

Write each sentence and separate the name of the person addressed from the rest of the sentence. In two sentences you will need more than one comma.

1. Ellen please find my thimble.
2. Be careful Bob not to lose your way.
3. There is no time to waste children.
4. This garden Uncle Tom belongs to me.

# IMPROVING WHAT YOU WRITE

The authors of stories that you read in books and magazines are seldom satisfied with their first writing of a story. They read and criticize it themselves, and often ask others to criticize it. Then they re-write it again and again until they feel that the story is the best they can make it.

Before you attempt to hand in a story, edit it; that is, read it over, looking for weak spots and mistakes. The first time you read it, judge the story itself. Is it a story your friends will like? Are the events told in order? Does the conversation sound real?

The second time you might read it to see whether all sentences are complete. At a third reading, see whether you could use more interesting words in place of some words you have used. At the last reading, look for mistakes in spelling, punctuation, and capitalization.

As you plan, write, edit, and rewrite your story, keep the following standards in mind.

---

### STANDARDS FOR STORYWRITING

1. Have a clever title for the story.
2. Start the action at once in the opening sentence or two.
3. Tell the events in order.
4. Make your characters converse.
5. Plan a good ending.

---

## OTHER KINDS OF STORIES

If the class decided that your story of family life was a good one, you will enjoy writing other kinds of stories. If you did not succeed in writing a good story of family life, do not be discouraged.

Plan to have more story-writing periods. Follow the suggestions on this and the next page.

### Fantastic tales

It is fun sometimes to let your imagination run wild and have all sorts of impossible things happen in a story. What strange and fantastic tale can you imagine? You might go to the moon in a rocket, find a treasure chest on a lonely island, or slay a dragon. Stretch your imagination. Plan a story about a strange and unusual happening.

### Animal or nature stories

Perhaps you are fond of animals and like the outdoors. You might choose an animal or a bird about which you know a great deal, and write a story that brings out some of the creature's habits and traits. It might be a story about your experiences in training

a wild creature, or about your experiences in taking kodak pictures of wild life.

## Stories of travel

If you enjoy reading books that tell about travel in strange lands, you might like to write a story about a make-believe trip to a land you would like to visit. Perhaps you can tell of a trip in a jinrikisha in China, or a trip by camel train in Egypt. Let your knowledge of geography help your imagination.

Perhaps you might tell of an imaginary journey on a magic carpet to some far-off land of make-believe.

## Stories of adventure

You may enjoy writing stories that are full of excitement. They may be about a scary night at camp, a narrow escape while hunting or fishing, a fight with the Indians, a pioneer child's adventure while going on an errand through the deep forest, or some other exciting happening.

Perhaps some members of the class will think of other kinds of stories. As they are suggested, talk over each kind of story.

Plan a period each week for writing stories. Each of you can think of ideas for a story in your spare time. Write it in the story-writing period.

[ 261 ]

# WRITING A DESCRIPTION

A travel tale should have clearly worded descriptions. Think of good verbs and describing words that will bring pictures to the minds of your readers.

Read the paragraph below. See whether you can get a picture of what is described.

> The rickety wheels of the jinrikisha rattled over the cobbled pavement of the narrow street. The ragged coolie jogged on and on in a tireless trot, seeming not to mind the scorching rays of the noonday sun.

Which verb makes you hear a sound? Which makes you see how an action took place? Which describing word makes you feel the heat? Which word or words make you see some object clearly?

In each sentence below, supply a word, either a verb or a describing word, that will make the reader see or hear clearly:

1. The __?__ elephant rolled his __?__ eyes toward me.
2. As he knelt, I climbed up into the __?__ howdah on his back.
3. Soon he was __?__ his way through the __?__ jungle, while I was doing my best to keep my balance in the __?__ howdah.

## SHARING WHAT YOU WRITE

Sometimes you may write a story just to amuse yourself. Such stories you may want to put into a little booklet to take home. But most of the time you will want to share your stories with others. Several ways are suggested here. Discuss them in class and decide what you will do.

1. Read your stories to the class.

2. Let the bulletin-board committee post the best stories on the bulletin board.

3. Put them in a folder on the library table for all to read.

4. Make a class booklet of stories, poems, and plays.

5. Have each boy and girl make a little book of his own and put it on the library table.

6. Publish the best ones in the school newspaper.

7. Have a program where different members of the class share their stories, poems, and plays with other classes or guests who are invited to school.

# RHYTHM IN POETRY

Long ago, wandering musicians traveled about Europe. In England such a musician was called a minstrel, and he carried with him a musical instrument called a *lute*.

Wherever one of these wandering minstrels went, he received a hearty welcome, and he often stayed for days at the palace of a king or noble. Every evening the knights and ladies gathered about the minstrel in the great hall to hear him sing to the music of his instrument. Some of the songs told stories of heroes and of happenings in far places. These songs became known as *ballads*.

When the minstrel stopped to sing in the courtyard of a great manor or in a wayside village, the people gathered about him. As they listened, some of them joined in the chorus of the ballad; others danced, or tapped a foot, or clapped hands to the regular beat, or *rhythm*, of the lines of the song.

The lines of a poem have rhythm. Your teacher will read aloud the poem below. Notice how her voice naturally accents the words or syllables that have accent marks over them.

### I MET A GIANT

I mét a gíant ín the lané
  Who shook his físt at mé.
"Boó," said Í, "I'm nót afraíd."
  But nót a word said hé.

He gnashéd his teéth, he stampéd his foót,
  He triéd to frighten mé.
"Boó," I saíd, "I'm nót afraíd.
  You're just a windy treé!"

VALINE HOBBS

Here is a poem with a different rhythm. Listen for the accented syllables as your teacher reads it.

### MOVING

  I like to move.  There's such a feeling.
  Of hurrying
    and scurrying,
  And such a feeling
  Of men with trunks and packing cases,
  Of kitchen clocks and mother's laces,
  Dusters, dishes, books and vases,
  Toys and pans and candles.

[ 265 ]

I always find things I'd forgotten:
An old brown teddy stuffed with cotton,
Some croquet mallets without handles,
A marble and my worn-out sandals,
A half an engine and a hat . . .
And I like that.

I like to watch the big vans backing,
And the lumbering
    and the cumbering,
And the hammering and the tacking.
I even like the packing!
And that will prove
I like to move!

EUNICE TIETJENS

I. Did the rhythm of this poem make you hear the bump-bump of boxes and crates being pulled downstairs, and the rumble of the big moving wagons? Read some lines that make you feel the hurry of packing.

II. Name some rhyming words in the poem.

# PAINTING WORD PICTURES

If you were to tell someone about a snowfall, you might say, "Early last evening it began to snow. By morning the snow was very deep."

Read the following stanzas that show how a poet once told the same facts:

> The snow had begun in the gloaming,
>     And busily all the night
> Had been heaping field and highway
>     With a silence deep and white.
>
> Every pine and fir and hemlock
>     Wore ermine too dear for an earl,
> And the poorest twig on the elm tree
>     Was ridged inch deep with pearl.

From "The First Snowfall"
by JAMES RUSSELL LOWELL

Which word means *twilight?* Do you notice that *gloaming* has a softer and more musical sound than *twilight?* Why do you think the poet chose *highway* instead of *road?*

Can you think of a better way to describe the silence of a snowy morning than the last line of the first stanza?

Ask several girls and boys to describe the picture that the second stanza paints. See whether anyone gives a better description than the poet gave. Do you think the poet chose good picture-making words? Name some.

# USING COMPARISONS

This poem tells you how something looks or sounds
by comparing it to something else:

### DANDELION

O little soldier with the golden helmet,
What are you guarding on my lawn?
You with your green gun
And your yellow beard,
Why do you stand so stiff?
There is only the grass to fight!

HILDA CONKLING

Had you ever thought of a dandelion standing
straight and stiff as a soldier?   What is his helmet?
What is his gun?   Does the poem make you see a
company of dandelions on a lawn?

Read this short poem.   Be ready to tell the two
things that are compared.

### THE FOG

The fog comes
on little cat feet.

It sits looking
over harbor and city
on silent haunches
and then moves on.

CARL SANDBURG

When the poet compares the fog to a cat, does it
make you see how softly the fog creeps along?

[ 268 ]

# POEMS FOR FUN

A poem does not have to be serious. It may be merry and gay or tell about common, everyday things.

Read the following poem. Have you ever seen what the poem tells about?

### SUN AND MOON

The moon by night, the sun by day,
My storybooks and schoolbooks say,
And yet one early afternoon
Most certainly I saw the moon.
And wouldn't it indeed be fun
If some dark night I saw the sun?

ROSE FYLEMAN

Have you ever seen the moon in the daytime? Tell how it looked.

The poem on this page tells about an experience that every boy and girl must have had. Read the poem. It makes a common experience seem like fun.

### In Praise of Dust

Dust is such a pleasant thing —
A soft gray kind of covering
For furniture, whereon to draw
Letters and pictures by the score.
Why won't the grownups let dust stay,
Instead of brushing it away?

RACHEL FIELD

Have you ever thought it fun to write or to draw pictures on a dusty surface? Tell about it.

Perhaps you like some of the weeds that your father pulls up from the lawn or garden; or the leaves that lie on the ground, but are soon raked up and burned. Write a rhyme about them.

# A POEM OF YOUR OWN

It would be fun for you to try to write a poem of your own. Before you do it, think of what you noticed about some of the poems you have been reading in this unit. Here are some reminders:

1. In the first place, you discovered that a poem may tell about some everyday thing that you saw, or some little experience you enjoyed. So choose a simple experience as the subject of your poem.

2. Next, think of words that will make others see what you saw, or hear what you heard, or feel what you felt. Use such words in your poem.

3. Make your lines "keep time"; that is, make them have rhythm.

4. Make your lines rhyme if you wish; but not all poems have rhymes.

Do not think that writing a poem is a lesson. Do not try to write it at any special time. But the next time you see or do something that you enjoy very, very much, think how you might make someone else share your pleasure. Try to put into words just what you saw or felt.

If the poem does not suit you at once, keep thinking about it and working over the words and lines until you have a poem that will make others understand what you felt. Then, take the poem to school and read it to your class.

# Unit Nine

## A REVIEW UNIT

## THE STORY OF OUR FLAG

You probably know that our first national flag had thirteen red and white stripes and thirteen gleaming white stars. But did you know that the great naval hero, John Paul Jones, was one of the first to hoist the new flag? He flew the Stars and Stripes from his ship, the *Ranger*, on the Fourth of July, 1777.

The picture on the opposite page shows his flag receiving from the French fleet the first gun salute ever given our national flag. That moment must have stirred the hearts of John Paul Jones and his crew, just as it stirs ours today.

Have you ever stopped to think that our language, like our flag, has been handed down to us by men and women who loved America? Do you show respect for our language, as you do for our flag, by using it correctly at all times?

This book has given you many helps for improving your language. This unit will help you discover how much you have learned.

# REVIEWING CAPITAL LETTERS

Capital letters are used to call attention to special words and words used in special ways. When we begin a word with a capital letter, we say we have *capitalized* that word. On the following pages are listed many everyday rules for capitalization.

1. Capitalize the first word of a sentence.
   The French first saluted our flag in 1778.

2. Capitalize important parts of proper names.
   1. Persons, their titles, and initials:
      Mr. Franklin K. Lane

   2. Avenues, streets, cities, and states:
      2100 Idlewood Avenue
      Richmond 20, Virginia

   3. Days, months, and their abbreviations.
      Monday   Mon.        December   Dec.

   4. Holidays:
      Flag Day, June 14      Fourth of July

   5. Countries, peoples, and tribes:
      Brazil      Brazilians      Blackfeet Indians

   6. Buildings and monuments:
      Patrick Henry School
      Paul Revere Monument

   7. Organizations and clubs:
      The American Legion          The Pep Club

8. Businesses and services:
   Alt Milling Co.          The Forest Service
9. Mountains, rivers, ships, and flags:
   Pike's Peak              Half Moon
   Hudson River             Old Glory

3. Always capitalize the word *I*.

   When I group the flags, I place the Stars and
   Stripes in the center.

4. Capitalize the first and all important words in
titles of books, poems, and stories.

   "Makers of the Flag" (a story)
   *The Little Book of Flags* (a book)
   "The Flag Song" (a poem)

5. The first word in a line of poetry is usually
capitalized.

   If a task is once begun,
   Never leave it till it's done.

6. Capitalize the first word of each topic in an
outline or a list.

   I. Famous flags
      A. Flag of the ship, *Mayflower*
      B. Ensign hoisted by John Paul Jones

7. Capitalize the first word in the greeting and
closing of a letter.

   Dear Mary,        Sincerely,

   Gentlemen:        Very truly yours,

# REVIEW OF PUNCTUATION

Like capital letters, punctuation marks help to guide the reader.

1. Place a period after a sentence that makes a statement or gives a command.

> The Stars and Stripes fly overhead.
> Hoist the flag at sunrise.

2. Place a period after —
    1. abbreviations and initials.
    > Dr. A. E. Brown     Mrs. M. R. Wilson

    2. numbers and letters in outlines or lists.
    > Flags of Discovery
    > I. Spanish flag
    >   A. Carried by Columbus
    >   B. Raised at San Salvador

3. Place a question mark after a sentence that asks a question.

> Can you see Old Glory yet?

4. Place an exclamation point after a sentence that shows strong feeling.

> How proudly she flies!

5. Use an apostrophe to show —
    1. possession.
    > citizen's duty     forefathers' dream

   2. a missing letter in a contraction.
     Don't drag the flag.

6. Use a comma to set off —
   1. a city from its state.
     Flagstaff, Arizona    Joliet, Illinois

   2. the day from the year.
     June 14, 1777    February 12, 1809

   3. a word in direct address.
     Mr. President, may I make a motion?

7. Use a comma after the greeting of a friendly letter and after the closing of any letter.
   Dear Sara,       Your friend,
       Yours truly,

8. Use a colon after the greeting of a business letter.
   Gentlemen:      Dear Sir:

9. Enclose the exact words of a speaker in quotation marks. Capitalize the first word in the quotation. Set it off from the rest of the sentence with some mark of punctuation.
   He said, "Good morning, Old Glory."

10. Use a hyphen to break a word at the end of a line. Break between syllables.
   pro-cession    col-onies    democ-racy

## Practice with Capitalization and Punctuation

Trained writers capitalize and punctuate their material as they write it. They are also careful to check their work for mistakes.

1. Rewrite this story. Use capital letters and punctuation marks wherever they are needed.

john paul jones and the flag

john paul jones was a great american hero in 1775 he was appointed a naval commander

on the fourth of july he sailed to portsmouth new hampshire there he raised the stars and stripes over his ship on this occasion he said gentlemen this flag and i are twins we shall always float together

in 1778 he sailed for europe there his flag received a salute from a french ship this was the first foreign salute ever given to the new flag of the united states

2. Rewrite these sentences. Use capital letters and punctuation marks wherever they are needed.

1. the home of mrs betsy ross in philadelphia pennsylvania is a memorial
2. my father is a member of the american legion
3. a good book is *uncle sam's marines* by george avison
4. did captain robert gray discover the columbia river

[ 278 ]

3. Capitalize and punctuate these letter parts:

                    2026 orchid street
                    los angeles california
                    june 10 19—

exposition park museum
los angeles california
gentlemen

                    very truly yours

4. Capitalize the topics in this outline and use periods where necessary:

        I  early flags
           A  flags of discovery
           B  flags of the colonies

5. Capitalize and punctuate these sentences. Use apostrophes where necessary.

    1. dont place lettering on our countrys flag
    2. place the field of blue to the speakers right
    3. finlands flag is blue and white, isnt it

6. Read these famous old quotations before you copy them. You will need to use capital letters, quotation marks, and other kinds of punctuation marks to make them correct.

    1. benjamin franklin said  we must all hang together, or we shall all hang separately
    2. dont give up the ship  said captain lawrence as he lay dying

[ 279 ]

# WORD FORMS YOU KNOW

On the next five pages you will find help with word forms on which you were tested in earlier units.

You studied all these forms in the third and fourth grades. But you will want to review each one now before doing the practice exercises.

## Go; do; see; run; come

Study these verb forms before you rewrite the story below. Choose the correct form for each sentence.

| Now | Past Time | With a Helper |
|-----|-----------|---------------|
| go | went | have gone |
| do | did | has done |
| see | saw | had seen |
| run | ran | have run |
| come | came | has come |

### A FUNNY FOURTH

Have you ever (ran, run) to a Fourth of July picnic? I (did, done) once.

My brother and I had set out on our bicycles. Before we had (gone, went) a mile, I had a flat tire. Even if I had (run, ran), I could not have kept up with my brother. So he (went, gone) on ahead.

About that time a goat grazing along the road (saw, seen) me. Lowering his head, he (came, come) toward me. I hid my bicycle and (ran, run) all the way to the picnic.

## Forms of *is* and *are*

When you speak of one thing, say *is* and *isn't* for present time; *was* and *wasn't* for past time, as:

1. The flag *is* flying, *isn't* it?
2. Leif Ericson's flag *was* the Viking Raven, *wasn't* it?

When you speak of more than one thing, say *are* and *aren't*, *were* and *weren't*, as:

1. The flags *are* colorful, *aren't* they?
2. The banners *were* grouped, *weren't* they?

Always use *are* and *were* with the word *you*, as:

1. You *are* ready.    2. You *were* ready.

Write this conversation, using the correct forms:

"You boys (were, was) in the parade, (wasn't, weren't) you, Alec?" asked Ben.

"We (was, were) flag-bearers," said Alec.

"(Isn't, Aren't) the flagstaffs heavy?" asked Joan.

"You (are, is) correct," replied Alec.

## I; me

When it is right to use *I* alone, it is right to say *You and I* or *Kay and I*.  When it is right to use *me* alone, it is right to say *You and me* or *Kay and me*.

Choose the correct forms:

1. Sue and (I, me) wanted a flag.
2. Father gave one to Sue and (I, me).

[ 281 ]

## Can; may

*Can* means *able to*. *May* is used *to ask* or *grant permission*. Choose the correct forms:

1. (May, Can) I go to the rally, Mother?
2. (Can, May) you play a bugle, Ted?
3. Mother said I (may, can) go.

## Well; good

*Well* describes the action of a verb; *good* describes a person or thing. Choose the correct forms:

1. The play is (good, well).
2. Dave acted his part (good, well).
3. Ann played (well, good) enough to win.

## Any; no

Never use *no* with words ending in *n't*. Choose the correct forms:

1. The English flag hasn't (any, no) stars.
2. There wasn't (any, no) place for us.

## Wrote; ate

Always use a helping word with the verb form *written* or *eaten*.

Rewrite these sentences, using the correct forms:

1. Have you (wrote, written) your story yet?
2. We had (ate, eaten) our lunch early.
3. Ann had (wrote, written) her story before she (et, ate) her lunch.

[ 282 ]

### Drew; drawn

Always say *drew*. Never say "drawed." Always use a helper with *drawn*. Choose the correct forms:

1. We (drew, drawed) a picture of the flag.
2. Have you (drawn, drew) a picture of the American flag?
3. They (drew, have drew) names for the prize.

### Let; leave

*Let* means *allow*; *leave* means *go away* or ·*allow to remain*. Choose the correct forms:

1. (Let, Leave) me blow your bugle.
2. (Leave, Let) your flag with me.
3. Mother will (let, leave) me go to the parade.

### Those; them

Remember that *those* points out persons or things. Fill the blanks with *those* or *them:*

1. __?__ sailors were brave.
2. Our nation should honor __?__.
3. __?__ children will sing for __?__.

### Unnecessary words

Each of these sentences has an unnecessary word in it. Rewrite the sentence correctly:

1. Sam Houston he traveled to Washington.
2. Some Cherokee Indians they went with him.
3. The Congress it decided to move the Cherokees west of the Mississippi River.

[ 283 ]

### Knew; known

Do you always say *knew*, remembering that there is no such word as "knowed"? Do you always use a helper with *known*? Choose the correct forms:

1. I have (known, knowed) the story of Betsy Ross and the flag for a long time.
2. I (knew, knowed) it before I started to school.
3. How long have you (known, knowed) "America the Beautiful"?
4. The author of that song (knew, knowed) and loved America.

### Doesn't; don't

Say *he* or *it doesn't*. Say *I* or *they don't*. Choose the correct forms:

1. (Don't, Doesn't) the story of John Paul Jones thrill you?
2. All books (don't, doesn't) tell the same stories about him.
3. As long as you enjoy the stories, I (doesn't, don't) care how long you keep the book.

### Learn; teach

You *learn* how to display the flag, but someone *teaches* you how to do it. Choose the correct forms:

1. (Teach, Learn) me how to hoist the flag?
2. I am sure I can (teach, learn) if you will (learn, teach) me.

# A REVIEW ROUNDUP

Most of the word forms you have just reviewed are used in this story about early settlers in Virginia. Choose the correct forms as you read each sentence:

When white men first (came, come) to Virginia, they (saw, seen) many turkeys. These birds (ran, run) wild in the forests as they had (did, done) for hundreds of years.

After the settlers had (eaten, ate) some of the turkey meat, they decided it was very (good, well). But they hadn't (any, no) grain to plant.

"The Indians (is, are) friendly," said Captain John Smith. "(Let, Leave) us ask them for help. They can (teach, learn) us many useful things."

After the men had (gone, went) to the Indians for help, they learned to plant maize, or corn. It grew very (good, well).

Captain Smith wrote to a friend in England. This is what he had (wrote, written):

"I have always (known, knew) that brave men (don't, doesn't) give up easily. Our men (are, is) afraid of nothing. Some have sailed with me while I have (drawn, drew) maps of the New England coast."

Copy this story, using the correct forms in each sentence. Exchange your paper with a classmate. Be sure to correct any mistakes he marks.

# REVIEWING NEW WORD FORMS

During the year you learned the correct forms of a number of words you did not study in the earlier grades. Here are review exercises on these forms.

## Gave; given

1. Choose the correct form in each sentence below. Turn to page 234 if you need help.

1. We have (gave, given) the flag salute.
2. We (gave, given) it at assembly.
3. Have you (given, gave) it recently?
4. Bob has (gave, given) me a flag.

2. Write two complete sentences. Use *gave* in one and *given* in the other.

## Began; begun

1. Choose the correct form in each of the sentences below. Turn to page 58 if you need help.

1. I have (begun, began) a story about Paul Revere.
2. Paul Revere (begun, began) his famous ride on the evening of April 18, 1775.
3. Had the Revolutionary War (began, begun) before he made his ride?
4. Have you (began, begun) to enjoy the stories about our American heroes?

2. Write two complete sentences. Use *began* in one and *begun* in the other.

*Say; said*

1. Choose the correct form in each of the following sentences. Turn to page 56 if you need help.

   1. "Let's have a flag quiz," (says, said) Tim to the Boosters Club one day. "How many red stripes does our flag have?"
   2. "I (says, say) seven," (said, says) Dave.
   3. "I (says, say) six," (says, said) Mary.
   4. "Did you (say, said) six or seven, Dave?" asked Tim.
   5. "I (says, said) seven. Am I right?" asked Dave.

2. Write two sentences. Use *say* in one and *said* in the other.

*Sit; sat*

1. Choose the correct form in each of the following sentences. If you need help, turn to page 235.

   1. He (sit, sat) forward in the saddle like a cowboy.
   2. I like to (sit, sat) in the saddle.
   3. My little brother (sit, sat) in front of me.
   4. Did you know that a coyote (sit, sat) on a hilltop watching us?
   5. Will your dog (sit, sat) up and beg?
   6. (Sit, Sat) down beside me.

2. Write two sentences. Use *sit* in one and *sat* in the other.

## Spoke and spoken; broke and broken

Choose the correct form in each of the following sentences. Turn to page 215 for help.

1. The flag has (spoke, spoken) to the Flagmaker.
2. Has the flag ever (spoke, spoken) to vou, as it did to the Flagmaker?
3. Fred has (broken, broke) the rules for displaying the flag.
4. If you had (broke, broken) the rules, what would you have done?
5. The Mayor has (spoken, spoke) to us about the meaning of Flag Day.
6. He (spoke, had spoke) to us before about other things.

## Took and taken

Choose the correct form in each of the following sentences. Turn to page 215 if you need help.

1. Do you know when our flag was first (took, taken) around the world?
2. The good ship *Columbia* (took, taken) it in 1790.
3. Old Glory was (taken, took) into Africa in 1871 by Henry M. Stanley.
4. In 1813 Commodore Porter (took, taken) our flag around Cape Horn.
5. Do you know of other interesting places where our flag has been (took, taken)?

[ 288 ]

## Grew and grown; threw and thrown

In each of the following sentences, choose the correct form. Turn to page 104 for help.

1. Our country has (grown, grew) a great deal in the past two hundred years.
2. The number of stars in the flag (growed, grew) from 13 to 48.
3. The sailors of the *Ranger* (threw, throwed) the anchor overboard.
4. I have never (thrown, throwed) a rock at a bird.
5. Has the population of your city (growed, grown) during the past year?
6. Harry has (threw, thrown) his lariat over the calf's head.

## Flew and flown; blew and blown

In each of the following sentences, choose the correct form. Turn to page 104 for help.

1. The wind has (blowed, blown) the flag to tatters.
2. The American flag has (flown, flew) from a schoolhouse in Massachusetts since 1812.
3. When the bugle has (blew, blown), the flag will be (flew, flown).
4. The electric fan (blew, blowed) the flag in a straight line.
5. The Dutch flag was (flown, flew) from the mast of Henry Hudson's ship.

[ 289 ]

## Sang and sung; rang and rung

Answer each question below with a complete sentence. Be sure to use the correct form of the verb in your sentence. Turn to page 187 if you need help.

1. Has your class sung "The Star-Spangled Banner" or "America" this week?
2. Has the class bell rung yet?
3. Do you know who rang it?
4. Have you ever rung the fire bell?
5. Have John and Mary sung their Flag Day songs?
6. When the class bell has rung, will the class sing?

## Set and sit

1. Turn to page 239 before you choose the correct forms for these sentences:

1. If you (set, sit) the alarm clock, we shall get up in time to see the parade.
2. Did you help your mother (set, sit) the table for your party?
3. Shall I (sit, set) in the front row?
4. (Set, Sit) the flowers where we can all see them.
5. We shall all (sit, set) together.
6. Why does the sun always (set, sit) in the west?

2. Write two complete sentences. Use *set* in one and *sit* in the other.

[ 290 ]

## A and *an*

Are you always careful to use *a* and *an* correctly? Turn to page 149 if you need help.

Write these sentences, using the correct forms:

1. We found (a, an) flag in the attic.
2. Why is (a, an) eagle our national emblem?
3. The Dutch flag had (a, an) orange, a blue, and a white stripe.
4. (An, A) explorer first carried Old Glory beyond the Arctic Circle.

## A REVIEW ROUNDUP

Rewrite these paragraphs, using the correct forms:

### A FLAG DAY PROGRAM

Did you (set, sit) where you could see the program? After the assembly bell (rang, rung), the program (began, begun) with a song. We had never (sang, sung) the song before, but we (did, done) fairly well.

The flag was (took, taken) to the platform while the bugler (blew, blowed) his bugle. The audience had (growed, grown) very still. The silence was (broke, broken) by the principal. The flag (threw, throwed) a shadow across her face. Before she had (spoke, spoken) very long, another flag was (flown, flew) from the school flagpole.

# REVIEWING NOUNS

During the year you reviewed the things you already knew about *nouns*, or name words, and you also learned several new things about them.

1. You learned that all nouns are classed as *common* or *proper*. Common nouns are written with small letters, but the first letter of a proper noun or important part of one, is capitalized, as:

| *Common* | *Proper* |
|---|---|
| flag | Stars and Stripes |
| war | Revolutionary War |
| battle | Battle of Bunker Hill |

2. You learned that nouns have *singular* and *plural* forms. Nouns form their plurals in several different ways, as:

| *Singular* | *Plural* |
|---|---|
| banner | banners |
| seaman | seamen |
| mass | masses |

If you are not sure how to form the plural of any noun, your dictionary will help you.

3. You learned that both singular and plural nouns show ownership, or *possession*. The apostrophe and *s* or the apostrophe alone are signs of possession, as:

| *Singular* | *Plural* |
|---|---|
| George Washington's flag | the colonies' flag |
| John Paul Jones's flag | the minutemen's flag |

These exercises will help you test your knowledge of nouns. Be sure to capitalize all proper nouns.

1. Write the headings *Common* and *Proper* on a sheet of paper. List these common nouns:

| | | | |
|---|---|---|---|
| star | ship | river | mountain |
| explorer | battle | general | organization |

Think of a proper noun to match each common noun and place it in the *Proper* column.

2. Write the plural of each of these common nouns. Turn to page 155 if you need help.

| | | | |
|---|---|---|---|
| sheep | child | committee | history |
| stripe | class | factory | chairman |

3. Turn to pages 157–158 for help in writing possessives.

4. Rewrite each of these sentences. Use the apostrophe or apostrophe and *s* to make the words in parentheses show possession.

1. It is said that (John Paul Jones) flag was made from some young (ladies) dresses.
2. (Betsy Ross) home is now a museum.
3. Did you know that the American flag flies over (Francis Scott Key) grave?

5. Use the apostrophe or the apostrophe and *s* to write these expressions in shorter ways:

the banner of the boys
the bugle of James
the platform of the speaker

[ 293 ]

# WORKING WITH WORDS

Your language may be correct in every way and still fail to hold the interest of your reader or listener. Unless you use lively and meaningful words, your sentences will be dull.

In the books you read, the radio programs and the conversations you hear are thousands of words, ready and waiting to help you express your ideas in a clear and lively way.

What are you doing to make these words yours?

## Making words your own

All during the year you have been adding to your stock of words. You have been looking up the meanings of new words in your dictionary. You have been learning how to spell and pronounce correctly new and old words alike.

Study these words or groups of words that are used in connection with the flag:

| | |
|---|---|
| halyards | mast of a ship |
| flagstaff | run up a flag |
| flag unfurled | union of a flag |
| gun salute | strike a flag |
| flagship | reviewing stand |
| hoist a flag | flag at half-mast |

If you are not sure of the meaning of any expression, look it up in your dictionary.

Then use each one in a sentence of your own.

## Making word pictures

After you have turned to the picture on page 272, look at the underlined words in this sentence:

The <u>black-mouthed</u> cannon on the Admiral's <u>flagship</u> <u>roared</u> a <u>nine-gun</u> salute.

Is *black-mouthed* a good describing word? What does *nine-gun* tell you? What picture does the noun *flagship* bring to your mind? Does the verb *roared* help you hear the sound the cannon made?

1. Find a better word for each of the underlined nouns in these sentences. The suggestions below each sentence will help you.

Write the sentence, using the word you have chosen to replace the underlined word.

1. The United States emblem is a <u>bird</u>.
   (turkey, crow, eagle, robin)

2. Abraham Lincoln lived in a <u>house</u> on the prairie.
   (cottage, log cabin, palace)

3. Columbus crossed the ocean in a <u>boat</u>.
   (canoe, sailing ship, lifeboat, steamship)

2. Replace the underlined verbs in these sentences with words that bring pictures to your mind.

1. The buffalo herd <u>ran</u> through the pass.
   (hurried, galloped, thundered)

2. Ahead of the herd <u>went</u> the stagecoach.
   (rolled, lurched, rattled, whirled)

[ 295 ]

# MATCHING SENTENCE PARTS

This year you learned that every complete sentence must have a part that names and a part that tells, as:

Robert Fulton | invented the steamboat.

1. Below you will find sentence parts that name and other parts that tell. Match these parts so that they will make complete sentences about five great Americans. Use an encyclopedia if you need help.

| *Parts That Name* | *Parts That Tell* |
|---|---|
| 1. J. Edgar Hoover | 1. founded Philadelphia. |
| 2. Clara Barton | 2. opened the Northwest. |
| 3. Thomas Jefferson | 3. organized the Red Cross in America. |
| 4. William Penn | 4. was a great president. |
| 5. George Rogers Clark | 5. is Director of the FBI. |

2. Write each sentence. Draw a line between the naming part and the telling part.

1. Roger Williams made friends with the Indians.
2. The Indians gave him a large piece of land.
3. He and his followers built a town.
4. They called the new town Providence.

3. Write three complete sentences about any one of these great Americans: Thomas Edison, Cyrus McCormick, Sacajawea, Robert E. Lee, Helen Keller.

Be sure each sentence has a part that names and a part that tells.

# WRITING COMPLETE SENTENCES

If your sentences have naming and telling parts, they are complete. Which of the groups of words below is a complete sentence? Which is not?

1. If you protect our wildlife.
2. You are a good American if you protect our wildlife.

Read these groups of words. Find the incomplete sentences. Make a complete sentence of each one.

1. When white men first came to America.
2. The early settlers killed buffaloes for food.
3. Killed antelope and elk for their horns.
4. Today every state has game laws.


## COMBINING SENTENCES

Notice how Tom combined two of his sentences:

1. I joined the Cub Scouts. I was nine years old.
2. When I was nine, I joined the Cub Scouts.

Study these pairs of sentences. Combine each pair with the connecting word suggested. Place a comma after a beginning clause.

(after)    1. The bell rang. We went to assembly.

(while)    2. The band was playing. The flag was flying.

(because)  3. I enjoyed the program. Everyone knew his part.

[ 297 ]

# PARAGRAPH PUZZLES

A paragraph is a group of complete sentences about one main topic.

If you remember all the rules for capitalization and punctuation, and are on the alert for misspelled words, you will enjoy solving these paragraph puzzles. Take time to do each puzzle carefully.

## Editing a paragraph

1. In the paragraph below there are nineteen mistakes. Study the paragraph until you have found them all. Then write the paragraph, correcting each mistake.

general john c fremont was one of americas greatest explorers. While he was mapping the rocky mountains in 1841, he maid a flag to show the Indians that he wanted peace. on the flag was a eagle. In one claw it held a bunch of arrows, and in the other it held a piece pipe. do you think the indians understood what fremonts flag meant

2. Try to think of a good title for this paragraph about one of America's greatest explorers. Be sure to write the title correctly.

3. Ask a classmate to check your paragraph for you. If he points out errors you did not see, rewrite your paragraph.

Turn to pages 274–277 if you need more help.

## Outlining paragraphs

In reading stories and articles, you will usually find that each paragraph is written about one main topic with one or more subtopics.

Read these two paragraphs about an early flag:

### AMERICA'S OLDEST FLAG

The oldest flag in America is one that came from Spain. It was brought here by the Spanish explorer, Cortez, in 1519. After his victory, he gave it to his Mexican friends. It now lies under glass in the National Museum of Mexico City.

What a picture this flag must have made as it billowed its full ten feet under a blue Mexican sky! It was made of rich red satin. On the front side was embroidered a religious picture in blue and green. On the back were painted marks of Spanish royalty.

After you have read these paragraphs carefully, fill in the two subtopics under each main topic:

America's Oldest Flag
  I. Where the flag came from
     A.
     B.
 II. What the flag looked like
     A.
     B.

Turn to page 174 if you need help in outlining.

# STICKING TO THE TOPIC

In each of these paragraphs is a sentence which does not stick to the topic.

One of the great western heroes is General Custer, or Yellow Hair, as the Indians called him. A regular Army officer, Custer fought the Indians in Montana and the Dakotas after the Civil War. He was born at New Rumley, Ohio. At this time the Indian chiefs, Sitting Bull, Crazy Horse, and Rain-in-the-Face, were leading their braves in battle against the white settlers.

For many years Custer outwitted the Indians. Then, in June, 1876, he was ordered to the Big Horn River with a command of 208 men. Custer also fought during the Civil War. Custer and his men were suddenly surprised by a great band of Sioux Indians, under the leadership of Sitting Bull. The Indians massacred every man.

1. Copy the two sentences that do not stick to the topic in these paragraphs.

2. Read over this list of topics. Write two or more paragraphs about one that interests you. Use an encyclopedia. Be sure to stick to the topic.

    1. A flag story, as "Who Named Old Glory?"
    2. Your state seal, flag, flower, or motto
    3. A faraway flag (Dutch, Swedish)

# INDEX

*A* and *an*, using, 149, 163, 165, 191, 207, 234, 291
Abbreviations, writing, 36–37, 43, 153, 227
Accent marks, 34, 175, 265
Actors, standards for, 217
Addresses, writing, 186, 226, 228–230, 244–245
"Ain't," 70
Alphabetical order, in:
  card catalogues, 142
  dictionaries, 35
  encyclopedias, 137, 139, 163, 165
  names, 14, 121, 153, 171, 197
"And" habit, the, 76, 148, 238
Announcements, making, 199–200
*Any* and *no*, 103, 282, 285
Apostrophes:
  with contractions, 43, 191, 277, 279
  with possessives, 43, 157–158, 191, 276, 279
*Ate, eaten*, 70, 103, 282, 285

*Began, begun*, 58, 88, 90, 123, 167, 190–191, 207, 234, 286, 291
Blanks, filling, 41, 159
*Blew, blown*, 104–105, 125, 127, 151, 191, 207, 234, 289, 291

Book:
  lists, 52, 136, 150–151, 171, 189
  parts, 6
  reports, 42, 144–148
  standards for, 146
  reviews, 150, 152–153, 162, 167
Books:
  arrangement of, 14
  class, 76, 184, 188
  history of, 129–133, 136
  reference, 143
  standards for handling, 6
Breve, 134–135
*Broke, broken*, 215, 218, 219, 234, 288, 291
*Brought*, 70
*Burst*, 70

*Can* and *may*, 103, 282
Capitalizing:
  first word in a line of poetry, 275
  first word in a quotation, 86–87, 123, 188, 277, 278, 279
  first word in a sentence, 9, 12, 36, 38, 42, 76, 79, 127, 184, 201, 214, 274, 278, 279, 298
  *I*, 275
  in letters, 127, 186, 226–227, 229–230, 237, 241, 250–251, 275, 279

[ 301 ]

Capitalizing (*Continued*):
  in outlines, 57, 88, 174, 275, 279
  proper names, 36, 40, 42, 127, 151, 184, 186, 214, 218, 235, 274–275, 278, 279, 298
  titles, 36, 42, 57, 76, 127, 151, 171, 214, 259, 274, 275, 278, 298
Card, library, 159
Catalogue, card, using, 142–143, 170
Chairman:
  of a committee, 117, 199–200, 202–204
  of a meeting, 53, 196, 219
Check questions on:
  book reports, 146
  business letters, 229
  class library, 13
  conversation, 5, 106
  discussion, 15
  friendly letters, 237
  reading stories, 54–55
  speaking habits, 60, 148
  written lessons, 36
Check Tests, 20, 42, 43, 73, 103, 162, 205
Class activities:
  books, 76, 184, 188, 263
  bulletin board, 13, 41, 53, 221, 263
  campfire, 75
  club, 195–200
  conversation, 100
  folder, 210–213
  hospitality committee, 117
  letters, 162, 226
  library, 13–14
  post office, 238

programs, 69, 160, 189, 263
Story Hour, 53, 263
storywriting period, 261
Clauses, setting off beginning, 83, 89, 297
Club, conducting a, 195–200
Colon, using, 186, 226–227, 277, 279
*Come, came*, 20, 280, 285
Comma:
  in letter parts, 226–227, 230, 236, 241, 250–251, 277, 279
  to set off beginning clauses, 83, 89, 297
  to set off city from state, 277, 278
  to set off day from year, 36, 277
  to set off quotation, 86–87, 123, 188, 277
  to set off words of address, 258, 277, 278
Committees:
  planning work for, 203
  standards for, 202
  working on, 13, 14, 41, 53, 76, 116, 170, 188, 199, 202, 204, 210–212, 216, 240, 263
Comparisons in poetry, 268
Connecting words, using, 82–83, 84, 89, 91, 123, 297
Contractions, writing, 43, 191, 277
Conversation:
  class, 5, 93–103, 106, 144–145, 193–195, 221–224
  in stories, 54, 256
  standards for, 106
  table, 108–109

[ 302 ]

telephone, 119–122
with callers, 116–118
writing, 86–87
    standards for, 87
Courtesy:
    at table, 108–109
    in club work, 198–199, 206–207
    in conversation, 102, 106, 110–113
    in greetings, 112–113
    in letters, 186, 223, 227, 229, 243
    in the library, 143
    in telephoning, 120, 203
    with callers, 116–117
Cross-referencing in encyclopedias, 138

"Dandelion," by Hilda Conkling, 268
Description, writing, 262, 267
Dialogue, writing, 61, 69, 216
Dialect, 50, 54, 59, 71
Dictation, taking, 127, 251
Dictionary, using a, 7, 13, 21, 34–35, 39, 59, 132, 134–135, 154, 155–156, 175, 228, 231, 235, 245, 246, 294
*Did, done*, 20, 280, 285, 291
Direct address, words in, 258, 277, 278
Directions, giving, 110–111, 248
Directory, telephone, using a, 121, 230
Discussions:
    class, 5, 13, 15, 50, 53, 59, 69, 70, 73, 75, 76, 99,
108, 109, 133, 195, 204, 256, 263
    club, 202, 208–209
    committee, 202–204
    standards for, 15
*Doesn't, don't*, 205, 284, 285
Dramatizations, 61–69, 115, 117, 118, 121, 204, 216–217, 263
Drawing, 41, 76, 188, 210, 212
*Drew, drawn*, 162, 283, 285

Editing written materials, 12, 20, 38, 42, 79, 84–85, 127, 151, 153, 154, 167, 188, 210, 259, 298
Election of club officers, 196–197
Encyclopedia, using an, 13, 137–138, 296, 300
Envelopes, addressing, 186, 228, 230, 238
Exclamation point, using the, 8–10, 43, 86, 276
Explanations:
    giving, 182–183
    standards for, 182

Facts:
    gathering, 203
    reading for, 136–143, 170–172, 179
    writing for, 186
File:
    book-review, 153
    card, 142–143, 170
    picture, 143
"First Snowfall, The," by James Russell Lowell, 267

*Flew, flown,* 104, 125, 126, 151, 190, 207, 234, 289, 291

"Fog, The," by Carl Sandburg, 268

Folder, making a, 210–213

*Gave, given,* 234, 250, 251, 286

*Good* and *well,* 103, 282, 285

Greetings:
  letter, 186, 227, 229, 275, 277, 279
  social, 112, 113

*Grew, grown,* 104–105, 125, 126, 151, 191, 207, 234, 289, 291

Guide:
  cards, 153
  words, 35, 59, 139

Handwriting, 36, 227, 229, 237

Headings for:
  letters, 226, 229
  written lessons, 36–37

Holidays and festivals, studying, 169–178, 179–180, 184–186, 189

Homonyms, 21, 39, 154, 228

*Hurricane's Children, The,* by Carl Carmer, 45–49, 77–78

Hyphen, using, 245, 250–251, 277

*I* and *me,* 103

"I Met a Giant," by Valine Hobbs, 265

"In Praise of Dust" by Rachel Field, 270

Index, using an, 6, 171, 172

Initials, writing, 43, 274, 276

Integration with other subjects:
  citizenship, 273–300
  general, 1–4
  health habits, 203–206
  hobbies, 93–99
  reading, 7, 13, 45–49, 51–53, 69, 129–133, 150, 160–161, 238, 294
  social studies, 169–171, 176, 180

Introducing:
  persons, 116–118
  speakers, 206–207

Invitations, writing, 69, 248–249

*Is* and *are,* forms of, 70, 73, 281, 285

Judging:
  book reports, 147
  conversations, 106, 119–120
  discussions, 15, 53
  dramatizations, 115, 216–217
  expressions of parliamentary procedure, 219
  letters, 186
  stories, 53, 54–55, 256
  voices, 7

*Knew, known,* 205, 284, 285

Labels, making, 240

Layout, making a, 210–211

*Learn* and *teach,* 205, 284, 285

*Let* and *leave,* 162, 283, 285

Letters:
  business, 222, 226–227, 229–230, 242–243

standards for, 229
editing, 230, 250
friendly, 222–223, 236–237, 238
standards for, 237
of invitation, 69, 248–249
of request, 162, 186, 226
order, 222, 242–243
parts of, 226–227, 229, 236–237, 241, 275, 277
"thank-you," 223, 241

Library:
aids, 142–143
classroom, 13–14, 137, 170, 188, 263
public, 52, 137, 150, 159, 170–171
school, 52, 137, 142–143, 150

Listen, learning to, 7, 16, 70, 77–78, 206, 265–270, 294

Lists, making, of:
book, 150–151, 170
committee members, 13, 53
conversation topics, 100
holidays, 170
questions, 203, 206–207
rules, 55, 76, 115

Macron, 134–135
Magazines, reading, 41, 96, 150, 238, 242
Margins, correct:
in letters, 225, 226–227, 229, 237
in written lessons, 36
in written stories, 76
Messages:
delivering, 114–115
telephone, 120–121, 124, 203

Minutes, club, 200–201
Motions, making, 208–209, 219
"Moving," by Eunice Tietjens, 265–266

Newspapers, writing for, 162, 263
reading, 41
Notebook, Language, 18, 21, 34, 52, 150, 175, 214, 230
Notes, taking, 171, 172–174, 200–201, 203
Nouns:
capitalizing proper, 36, 40, 42, 127, 151, 184, 186, 214, 218, 235
common and proper, 40, 42, 184, 235, 274, 292–293
possessive, 43, 157–158, 164, 166, 191, 276, 292–293
singular and plural, 155–158, 164–166, 231, 292–293
Numbers:
in outlines, 57, 88, 90, 276
zone, 226–227

Oral skills. *See the following individual entries:*
"And" habit, the
Announcements, making
Chairman
Check questions
Club, conducting
Committee, working on a
Conversation
Courtesy
Directions, giving
Dramatizations

Oral skills (*Continued*):
  Election of club officers
  Explanations, giving
  Greetings, social
  Introducing persons
  Judging
  Messages
  Motions, making
  Pronunciation
  Reading aloud
  Reports, oral
  Speaker, introducing a
  Speech, habits, good
  Speeches, making
  Story, telling
  Tales, telling
  Telephone, using the
  Usage, correct
  Voice, good speaking
  Vowels, sounding correctly
  Words and expressions
Outlining:
  a folder, 211
  a report, 174, 180, 184
  a story, 57, 88
  notes, 172–173
  practice with, 90, 275, 276, 279, 299

Packages, sending, 223, 233, 240
Paragraphs:
  in written conversation, 86–87
  indenting, 12, 36, 38, 76, 201, 227, 229, 298
  topics in, 38, 138, 140–141, 180, 184, 229, 298, 299, 300
  writing, 12, 38, 76, 79, 153, 161, 167, 246, 298, 300
Periods:
  after abbreviations, 36, 43, 276
  after numbers in outlines, 57, 88, 90, 276, 279
  at end of sentences, 10, 12, 36, 38, 43, 76, 79, 127
Pictures, studying, 69, 124, 132–133, 135, 138, 143, 197, 295
Plurals. *See* Nouns
Poetry:
  reading, 188, 189, 264–270
  writing, 188, 263, 270–271, 275
Possessives. *See* Nouns
Post office:
  class, 238
  visiting a, 224, 232–233
Postal cards, writing, 244–245
Postal notes, sending, 224, 233, 242
President of a club, 196–200
Pronunciation:
  correct, 18, 19, 70, 71, 122, 175, 205, 294
  helps in, 34, 60, 134–135
Punctuation marks. *See* Apostrophes, Colons, Commas, Exclamation points, Hyphens, Periods, Question marks, Quotation marks

Question marks, using, 9, 10, 43, 86, 276
Questions, answering, 110–111, 141

Quotation marks, 43, 86–87, 89, 91, 123, 188, 257

Radio:
  listening to the, 7, 70, 294
  programs, 69, 160
  script for, 61–69
*Ran, run,* 20, 280, 285
*Rang, rung,* 187, 189, 190, 207, 234, 290, 291
Reading:
  aloud, 7, 61, 70, 84–85, 115, 122, 160–161, 263, 266, 271
  for facts, 136–143, 170–172, 179
  for the story, 22–32, 45–49, 62–68, 129–132, 253–256
Reports:
  book, 42, 144–148
  committee, 204
  oral, 171, 176–178, 180
    standards for, 178
  written, 184–185
    standards for, 184
Rhyme in poetry, 266, 270–271
Rhythm in poetry, 264–271
Riddles, book, 160–161

*Said,* 17, 56, 88, 90, 123, 167, 191, 207, 234, 287
*Sang, sung,* 187, 189, 190, 207, 234, 290, 291
*Saw, seen,* 20, 280, 285
Secretary of a club, 196–201
Sentences:
  beginning in different ways, 82, 246
  combining, 82–83, 89, 91, 123, 297
  complete, 11, 36, 79, 84–85, 167, 237, 296, 297
  kinds of, 8–10
  standards for writing, 9
  understanding, 11, 12, 36, 77–79, 80–81, 89, 91, 167, 238, 296
  using, 5, 7, 11, 58, 59, 107
  writing, 11–12, 36, 43, 76, 81, 154, 184, 201, 258, 274, 276, 278
*Set,* 239, 250, 251, 290, 291
Silent letters, 135
*Sit, sat,* 235, 250, 251, 287
Skimming, 78, 138, 140–141
Speaker:
  introducing a, 206–207
  inviting a, 203
Speech habits, good, 19, 60, 70, 122, 148, 205
Speeches, making, 206–207
Spelling, correct, 18, 21, 34, 36, 39, 154, 155–156, 228, 229, 230, 231, 237 259, 294, 298
*Spoke, spoken,* 215, 218, 219, 288, 291
Standards for:
  actors, 217
  an explanation, 182
  an oral report, 178
  a written report, 184
  business letters, 229
  committee workers, 202
  conversation, 106
  discussions, 15
  friendly letters, 237
  giving a book report, 146
  handling a book, 6
  storytelling, 55
  storywriting, 259

Standards for (*Continued*):
telephoning, 120
writing conversation, 87
writing sentences, 9
written lessons, 36
Stationery, kinds of, 225, 229, 237
Story:
Hour, 53
judging a, 54–55, 256
reading a, 22–32, 45–49, 253–256
telling a, 33, 57, 69
standards for, 55
writing a, 72–73, 74–75, 76, 256, 259–262, 280
standards for, 259
Study skills. *See the following individual entries:*
Alphabetical order
Book
Books
Card, library
Catalogue, card
Check Tests
Cross-referencing in encyclopedias
Dictionary, using a
Directory, telephone, using a
Encyclopedia, using an
Facts, reading for
File
Guide cards and words
Index, using an
Layout, making a
Library aids
Listen, learning to
Lists, making
Magazines, reading
Notebook, Language
Notes, taking
Outlining
Pictures, studying
Reading for facts
Skimming
Tables of contents, using
Tests and Keyed Practice
Topics in note-taking
Vocabulary building
Written lessons, preparing
Subject, keeping to a, 15, 38, 101, 182, 184, 247, 300
"Sun and Moon," by Rose Fyleman, 269
Syllabication, 19, 34, 175, 245, 277

Tables of contents, using, 6, 76, 171, 172, 188
Tales:
discussion of, 50, 69
reading, 45–49, 51–52, 62–68, 70
telling, 75
writing, 72–74, 76
Telephone:
directory, 121, 230, 243,
using the, 119–121, 124, 203
standards for, 120
Tests and Keyed Practice, 88–91, 125–127, 163–166, 189–190, 218–219, 250–251
"Thank-you":
letter, 223, 241
speech, 206–207
*Those* and *them*, 162, 283
*Threw, thrown*, 104–105, 125, 126, 151, 191, 207, 234, 289, 291

[ 308 ]

Titles, writing, 36, 57, 76, 151, 153, 171, 172, 184, 259, 274, 275, 298

*Took, taken,* 215, 218, 219, 234, 288, 291

Topics in:

encyclopedias, 137–139, 163, 165

note-taking, 172

paragraphs, 38, 138, 140–141, 180, 184, 229, 298, 299, 300

reports, 180

stories, 57

Usage, correct:

*a, an,* 149, 163, 165, 191, 207, 234, 291

"ain't," 70

*any, no,* 103, 282, 285

*ate, eaten,* 70, 103, 282, 285

*began, begun,* 58, 88, 90, 123, 167, 190, 207, 234, 286, 291

*blew, blown,* 104–105, 125, 127, 151, 191, 207, 234, 289, 291

*broke, broken,* 215, 218, 219, 234, 288, 291

*brought,* 70

*burst,* 70

*can, may,* 103, 282

*come, came,* 20, 280, 285

*did, done,* 20, 280, 285, 291

*doesn't, don't,* 205, 284, 285

*drew, drawn,* 162, 283, 285

*flew, flown,* 104, 125, 126, 151, 190, 207, 234, 289

*gave, given,* 234, 250, 251, 286

*good, well,* 103, 282, 285

*grew, grown,* 104–105, 125, 126, 151, 191, 207, 234, 289, 291

*is* and *are,* forms of, 70, 73, 281, 285

*knew, known,* 205, 284, 285

*learn* and *teach,* 205, 284, 285

*let* and *leave,* 162, 283, 285

*ran, run,* 20, 280, 285

*rang, rung,* 187, 189, 190, 207, 234, 290, 291

*said,* 56, 88, 90, 123, 167, 191, 207, 234, 287

*sang, sung,* 187, 189, 190, 207, 234, 290, 291

*saw, seen,* 20, 280, 285

*set,* 239, 250, 251, 290, 291

*sit, sat,* 235, 250, 251, 287

*spoke, spoken,* 215, 218, 219, 288, 291

*those, them,* 162, 283

*threw, thrown,* 104–105, 125, 126, 151, 191, 207, 234, 289, 291

*took, taken,* 215, 218, 219, 234, 288, 291

unnecessary words, 162, 283

*went, gone,* 20, 280, 285

*wrote, written,* 103, 282, 285

*You were,* 70, 281

Verbs, correct forms of, 104, 126, 187, 215, 235, 239. *See also* Usage, correct

vivid, 239, 262

Vocabulary, building, 16, 18, 22, 33, 35, 39, 175, 219, 246, 294

Voice, good speaking, 5, 7, 15, 70, 101, 106, 120, 122, 148, 161, 178, 217

Vowels:
  *a* and *an* with, 149, 163,
    165, 191, 207, 234, 291
  sounding correctly, 60, 71,
    134–135

*Wasn't, weren't.* See *Is* and *Are*
*Well, good,* 103, 282, 285
*Went, gone,* 20, 280, 285
Words and expressions:
  avoiding overworked, 16,
    56, 107
  choosing exact, 5, 7, 178,
    182, 236–237, 239, 241,
    246, 259, 262, 267
  dialect, 50, 54, 59, 71
  learning new, 16, 33, 35, 59,
    175, 200, 219, 246
  unnecessary, 162, 283
Written lessons, preparing,
    36–37
Written skills. *See the follow-
    ing individual entries:*
  Addresses, writing
  Blanks, filling
  Book, reports, reviews
  Books, class
  Capitalizing
  Clauses, setting off begin-
    ning
  Connecting words
  Contractions
  Dialogue, writing
  Dictation, taking

Direct address, words in
Editing written materials
Envelopes, addressing
Folder, making a
Handwriting
Headings
Initials, writing
Invitations, writing
Labels, making
Letters
Margins
Minutes, club
Newspaper, writing for
Nouns
Numbers
Packages, sending
Paragraphs, writing
Poetry, writing
Postal cards, writing
Punctuation marks
Reports, written
Sentences
Spelling, correct
Story, writing
Tales, writing
Titles, writing
Usage, correct
Words and expressions
*Wrote, written,* 103, 282, 285

*You were,* 70, 281

Zone number, in letters, 226–
    227